BABY FOOD
IN AN INSTANT

**Healthy
Organic
Purees
from Your
Multi-Cooker**

TABITHA BLUE

CASTLE POINT BOOKS
NEW YORK

BABY FOOD IN AN INSTANT. Copyright © 2020 by St. Martin's Press. All rights reserved.
Printed in the United States of America. For information, address St. Martin's Press,
120 Broadway, New York, NY 10271.

www.castlepointbooks.com

The Castle Point Books trademark is owned by Castle Point Publishing, LLC.
Castle Point books are published and distributed by St. Martin's Press.

ISBN 978-1-250-27046-7 (trade paperback)
ISBN 978-1-250-27047-4 (ebook)

Design by Melissa Gerber
Production by Mary Velgos
Photography by Tabitha Blue except photos on pages 38, 40, 48, 53, 55, 71, 82, 85, 88, 111, 114,
132, 137, 149-151, 153-154, 157 and all illustrations used under license from Shutterstock.com

Our books may be purchased in bulk for promotional, educational, or business use.
Please contact your local bookseller or the Macmillan Corporate and Premium Sales Department
at 1-800-221-7945, extension 5442, or by email at MacmillanSpecialMarkets@macmillan.com.

First Edition: 2020

10 9 8 7 6 5 4 3 2 1

CONTENTS

BABY'S BEST START

We all want the best for our kids, especially when it comes to health and nutrition. So why not start with their first foods? Nothing compares to the fresh taste of meals we make at home, including our little ones' purees and finger foods. And it's reassuring to know exactly what's in the little airplane bites you're inching toward those toothless grins.

Wondering how you could ever muster the time and energy to make baby food from scratch? With *six* kids (including a set of twins), I completely understand! That's why I'm sharing this cookbook filled with smart, real-life solutions for creating delicious homemade foods for your baby in an instant. The secret: every recipe is designed for a multi-cooker, which means wholesome baby food, fast. Your baby will benefit from the nutritional power and fresh flavor of homemade baby food. You'll enjoy the satisfaction of giving your baby food you feel good about without tons of hands-on prep time stealing you away from snuggles.

THE HOMEMADE ADVANTAGE

I've enjoyed making baby food for all of my kids, feeling confident about the nutritional advantages and pure ingredients. Then my son Skylar came along and showed me a new benefit to homemade first foods. Although he has grown to be an eater—as in, he likes just about everything—that wasn't always the case.

When Skye was first old enough to start eating, I was excited to make homemade baby food for him. I slowly introduced different

$ $ $

SIMPLE SAVINGS

Although you may consider making homemade baby food priceless for your baby's health and development, it actually saves you money too. Homemade organic baby food is nearly 45 percent cheaper than store-bought organic, according to Mint.com.

foods, but no matter the taste or texture, he didn't want anything to do with it. It took a lot of attempts and adjustments (and patience!) to find what enticed him. A huge advantage of making homemade baby food, besides controlling the quality of ingredients and nutrition, is that you can adjust flavors based on your baby's palate. Just keep giving your child the opportunity to taste and try new flavors.

Exploring different tastes is part of the process of developing a healthy relationship with food. The American Academy of Pediatrics has found a link between the flavors and tastes introduced in infancy and the likelihood of children taking to them as they grow. Add to that the fact that the infant stage is when kids are most amenable to trying new foods and textures, and it makes perfect sense that we should aim to introduce our wee ones to fresh flavors and textures as soon as they're reaching for a spoon. Those first foods are so important!

JUST WHAT YOUR BABY NEEDS

Beyond customizing for your baby's taste, making homemade food allows you to meet any dietary needs. Each recipe throughout this book is categorized to make it easy to see at a glance all the delicious recipes your baby can enjoy. Freezer-friendly recipes are also marked so you can make the most of meal prep.

- DAIRY FREE
- VEGAN
- GLUTEN FREE
- VEGETARIAN
- NUT FREE
- FREEZER-FRIENDLY

MAKING ORGANIC CHOICES

When I first started making baby food, I bought organic for just about everything. While organic produce does come with a higher price tag than its conventional counterpart, it still costs less to make homemade baby food with organic produce than it does to purchase organic or any kind of store-bought baby food. Plus, you get peace of mind that you're purchasing produce grown without the use of hormones, GMOs, antibiotics, and pesticides.

But if staying 100 percent organic isn't realistic for your budget or your shopping experience, you can still make choices that protect your family from the biggest risks. Because I have a large family, I prioritize my organic purchases according to which foods may have the highest concentration of pesticides. For foods that have a peel or skin I'll be removing, I'm more inclined to save money and purchase conventional.

Thankfully, the Environmental Working Group (EWG) put together a list of what's called the Dirty Dozen (see page 7), which will tell you which produce is most impacted by pesticides. I use it as a resource to prioritize my organic shopping. I can also feel confident purchasing conventional fruits and veggies from the Clean Fifteen list (see page 7). But here's the thing: I'm also a proponent of supporting local farms and regionally grown foods, and that doesn't always come with an organic label.

If it comes down to purchasing conventional produce or not purchasing at all, it's much more important for me to offer fruits and vegetables than to skip them. Trusting the federal guidelines on the amount of pesticides food can harbor, I'll wash our food and let my family enjoy it.

If you're committed to organic but not sure what your budget allows, refer back to these lists as your little cheat sheet on where to prioritize your organic dollars. Either way, it's important for both us and our little ones to eat plenty of healthy fruits and vegetables, whether they are conventional or organic.

PRODUCE PRIORITIES

THE EWG DIRTY DOZEN LIST INCLUDES:

- Apples
- Celery
- Cherries
- Grapes
- Kale
- Nectarines
- Peaches
- Pears
- Potatoes
- Spinach
- Strawberries
- Tomatoes

THE EWG CLEAN FIFTEEN LIST INCLUDES:

- Asparagus
- Avocados
- Broccoli
- Cabbage
- Cantaloupe
- Cauliflower
- Eggplant
- Honeydew melon
- Kiwi
- Mushrooms
- Onions
- Papaya
- Pineapple
- Sweet corn
- Sweet peas (frozen)

BABY FOOD PREP MADE EASY

What I wish someone had told me before I started making baby food is that you don't need a whole bunch of fancy gadgets. In fact, you probably already have in your kitchen most of the tools used for the recipes in this book—assuming you either own a multi-cooker or plan to buy one. Below is a list of the tools that I recommend and use in prepping, cooking, and storing homemade baby food.

Multi-cooker (+ trivet, usually included with cooker)

Any multi-cooker will make homemade baby food so much faster and easier! The tips and recipes in this book were tested using a 6-quart multi-cooker. Cooking times may vary depending on your multi-cooker's make, model, and size. Check your instruction manual for hints on how to get the best results. You'll find more pressure-cooking tips on page 11.

Immersion blender, blender, or food processor

My family makes all of our baby food with the help of an immersion blender. For many of these recipes, once cooked, I can puree right in the pot and save time on cleanup. But a standard blender or food processor works great as well and makes a very smooth puree; you just need to let the cooked food cool a bit before transferring.

Masher

A masher is another little kitchen gadget that can work magic right in the pot, especially for the chunkier purees!

Round baking pan

With a round baking pan that fits inside the pot of your multi-cooker, you can make amazing frittatas, breads, rice, meat loaf, and more delicious stage-4 foods for your baby.

Sling

Fitting a pot holder into your multi-cooker's space could be awkward. For removing hot baking dishes, a sling comes in handy. While you can fashion a sling with aluminum foil, a silicone sling designed for a pressure cooker makes the task easier.

Egg molds

A silicone egg mold is a fun little tool you can use with your multi-cooker to make bite-size—or in this case, child-size—egg dishes. It can also be used to make mini muffins and other finger-food "bites," creating neat little portions that store so easily.

Other kitchen utensils

- Chef's knife
- Colander
- Cutting board
- Instant-read thermometer
- Large zip-top freezer bags
- Mason jars
- Measuring cups and spoons
- Silicone freezer trays or ice cube trays
- Spatula
- Steamer basket
- Tongs
- Vegetable peeler

GETTING TO KNOW YOUR MULTI-COOKER

New to pressure cooking or trying new ways to use your multi-cooker? The biggest key to keep in mind is that cooking is an art. It takes time to get to know any new tool, so don't be too hard on yourself. Have fun, learn, and enjoy the process. You'll be a multi-cooker pro in no time! These tips will get you started.

- When cooking with a multi-cooker, the cook time is usually figured on actual time at pressure. Remember, it takes a few minutes to get the pot up to pressure. Also, most recipes call for a venting time, which can be 5 to 10 minutes per recipe. Allow for this in your actual cooking time.

- In any pressure cooker, liquid is what makes cooking possible. Never cook without liquid. If liquid is not present, the multi-cooker will give you a burn signal and stop cooking.

- Get to know your pressure release valve. While it seems very simple, there is a position to vent and a position to seal. I have gotten them mixed up and wondered why the pot never came up to pressure (the valve wasn't sealed, so all of the steam escaped). Multi-cookers also have a float valve that pops up when the pressure is full and drops when it is safe to open the lid. Never open the lid when the valve is in the up position.

- *Natural release* is the term used for allowing your pressure cooker to let out steam without touching the release valve. Normally this process takes about 10 minutes before you can safely remove the lid.

- *Quick release* is the term used for manually moving the valve button to the release position so that steam is let out much more quickly. Usually this process takes 1 to 2 minutes before you can safely remove the lid.

- The exterior of your multi-cooker pot will get warm, so keep it away from curious children who may accidentally burn themselves.

MEAL PLANNING AND STORAGE

There are so many benefits to making baby food ahead of time. When it comes to preparing homemade purees, what seems like a little bit of food can go a long way. For example, one sweet potato typically makes about 8 servings, or 16 ounces, of baby food. And in the earliest stages of feeding, that can be 16 servings!

It's easy to make food in batches and freeze for later. The food that you freeze can be defrosted and used as needed. For the best storage and safe feeding later, keep these tips in mind.

Fridge or freezer? After you have made your purees, you can store them in the refrigerator in a sealed container for a few days. But the best method to store baby food is to freeze it. Once purees have cooled, transfer them to a silicone cube mold or ice cube tray with 1-ounce compartments, cover, and freeze for 24 hours. Once the cubes are solid, transfer them to a larger container or zip-top freezer bag. Label the storage container with the name of the puree and the date. Most purees store in the freezer for up to 6 months.

Get ready to serve. You can defrost cubes of frozen puree overnight in the refrigerator to use the next day. If you forget to plan ahead and need to reheat a puree, you can use the stovetop or the microwave in a pinch. Simply warm the cubes in a pot over low heat, or to defrost in the microwave, use a glass bowl and the microwave's defrost setting. The goal temperature for serving is just over room temperature, so the food should feel slightly warm, but not hot, when feeding your baby. Make sure to test it on yourself before offering it to your little one.

The same process works for prepped finger foods and family meals. Place frozen food in the refrigerator the night before (or a day or two before) you plan to use it. You can finish defrosting in the microwave or on the stovetop if needed.

Follow safety guidelines. Although these tips aren't specific to baby food, it's good to have reminders.

- Never leave food on the counter for more than 2 hours to defrost.
- You cannot reheat or refreeze food more than once. So once you thaw baby food, keep it in the refrigerator until ready to use.
- If you don't think your baby will eat all that you have thawed, place just the food you plan to serve at this meal into a small bowl. Once you begin spoon-feeding, bacteria from the mouth transfers from the spoon back to the bowl, making it unsafe to store the leftovers. You can always add more if you need to!

TOGETHER THROUGH THE STAGES

No matter the age of your little one, coming together to eat is such a great way to share a bonding moment. As a parent, it's easy to obsess or worry about the nutrients our kids are getting. But what about the developmental moments? Newborns crave cuddle time during those bottle- or breast-feeding moments; it provides a perfect opportunity to slow down and snuggle together. As our children grow older and we begin to introduce foods in stages, it's important to keep thinking about the *how* along with the *what*.

FIRST-YEAR CAUTIONS

While there are so many foods for your little one to enjoy, there are a handful of foods to avoid in your baby's first year:

- Honey or foods containing honey
- Cow's milk (foods made with milk, such as yogurts and cheeses, are fine)
- Added sugars and sweeteners
- Foods that can be choking hazards—whole nuts, grapes, hot dog slices, and hard foods

Something I've found is that when we've had a hard time introducing new foods, often it's because we put too much pressure on our babies or on ourselves. Take a breath and a step back from the "structured" part of feeding time and just have fun with your baby. They'll be more likely to try something new, and in turn enjoy the new food; plus it leads to a stronger bond in every stage.

When is the right time? There's an old adage that says "food before one is just for fun," although many doctors recommend starting food around six months of age. Really, it's about taking cues from your baby and trying different foods, keeping in mind the fun aspect. If they don't want it or aren't ready, don't stress. They'll get there.

Some signs that your little one is ready for food include:
- The ability to hold their head up when sitting
- Opening their mouth and leaning forward toward food
- Grasping for a spoon and moving it toward their mouth
- Cooing and following the path of food while you eat
- Signs of fussiness or hunger after bottle- or breast-feeding

If you're seeing any of these signs, go ahead and try solid foods. You can start by offering foods one or two times per day. Don't be surprised if your little one pushes the food out of their mouth when learning to handle solid foods. Your goal in the beginning is to introduce new textures and tastes, so keep offering it, but you never need to force it.

Where do I begin? No matter at what age you begin feeding your baby solid foods (anything besides formula or breast milk), you'll follow the basic stages as your little one learns how to eat. If you're wondering what stages 1, 2, 3, and 4 mean, don't worry—you're not alone. Here's a basic breakdown.

Stage 1 baby food: Start by spoon-feeding your little one a variety of thinly pureed fruits, vegetables, and grains. For those first tastes, it's recommended to stick to one puree at a time for a few days in a row. This way, if there happen to be any allergic or adverse reactions, you'll know which food to avoid. You'll find lots of great single-food puree choices starting on page 18. If any of the purees seem too thick, simply add a little of the reserved cooking water, breast milk, or formula and blend to create the desired consistency.

Stage 2 baby food: Stage 2 purees are where you can really start exploring flavor combinations by mixing fruit, vegetable, and grain purees—and even adding in some herbs and spices. It's important to use foods that have already been tested during stage 1, as it's more difficult to pinpoint an allergy if introducing multiple foods at once. With fun and fresh tastes, the stage 2 purees (starting on page 58) will still have a smooth texture but can be thicker than stage 1 purees.

Stage 3 baby food: The main difference between stage 2 and stage 3 is that you're now introducing soft, cooked, small chunks of food in the puree to give your baby practice in chewing and swallowing before moving on to finger, or table, foods. Stage 3 (beginning on page 94) offers lots of hearty meat, pasta, and grain multi-ingredient puree meals. It's a great time to think about how many of your own meals can be your baby's meals as well with a gentle pulse in the blender.

Stage 4 finger foods: At stage 4 (beginning on page 122), it's time to pack away the blender (until you want to whip up a smoothie; see page 150 for my favorite smoothie recipes). Now, you're going to be offering your baby soft, cooked foods. This is a fun stage where your baby can play with food while you play with flavors and textures. Another label often used for this stage is "table food," which basically just means smaller, cut-up versions of your own meal.

Whatever stage of feeding you're in, be sure to include your baby in family mealtimes. Have fun at the table—they'll learn most from watching you!

STAGE 1

SINGLE-INGREDIENT PUREES

MANGO PUREE

Makes 16 ounces • Prep time: 5 minutes • Pressure time: 4 minutes

Mangoes are a magical source of vitamins A and C and folate. The ripest fruits will have a little give when you squeeze gently. To encourage an adventurous sense of taste in your baby, try adding different spices—such as cinnamon, nutmeg, or even coriander and ground cumin—to your puree once you've cleared the first taste. You may find yourself sneaking a spoonful as you try fun flavor variations!

2 mangoes, peeled, halved, and pitted

½ cup water

1. Place the mangoes and water into the multi-cooker; secure the lid.
2. Cook on High Pressure for 4 minutes.
3. When the cook time is complete, turn off the multi-cooker. Use the quick release valve to release the pressure.
4. After the float valve drops, remove the lid carefully.
5. With a slotted spoon, remove the mangoes to a small bowl and let cool for 20 minutes. Save the water.
6. Using an immersion blender, puree the mixture, adding the reserved water as needed for the desired consistency.
7. Transfer the puree to a storage jar or container.

{ ## SUPER SNACK SECRET

Don't pack away the puree recipes when your baby moves into the world of solid foods! Instead, use them as creative ways to mix flavor and nutrition into plain Greek yogurt. It's a wholesome snack for anyone in the family. }

SWEET POTATO PUREE

Makes 24–32 ounces • Prep time: 5 minutes • Pressure time: 15 minutes

Known for their anti-inflammatory benefits, sweet potatoes are a great source of vitamins A and C and high in fiber for healthy digestion (and a happier baby!). This recipe makes a big enough batch that you can share with your baby—try adding it to your oatmeal or blending into smoothies and sauces for a nutrient boost. Cinnamon is a natural flavor partner for this puree.

1 cup water	2 large sweet potatoes, peeled and cut into ¼-inch-thick slices

1. Place the trivet into the multi-cooker; add the water.

2. Place the sweet potato slices on the trivet; secure the lid.

3. Cook on High Pressure for 15 minutes.

4. When the cook time is complete, turn off the multi-cooker. Let the steam release naturally for 10 minutes, then use the quick release valve to finish releasing the pressure.

5. After the float valve drops, remove the lid carefully.

6. With a slotted spoon, remove the sweet potatoes to a medium bowl and let cool for 20 minutes. Save the water.

7. Place the sweet potatoes into a blender jar or a food processor.

8. Add ½ to ¾ cup of the reserved water to the sweet potatoes. Blend the mixture, adding more water as needed for the desired consistency.

9. Transfer the puree to a storage jar or container.

{ ONE SWEET MESS }

In early baby food stages, you'll blend reserved cooking water or breast milk with sweet potatoes for a super-smooth puree. As your baby grows and masters the next food stages, mashed sweet potatoes make a great first finger food. Be prepared with a camera and lots of cleansing wipes!

APRICOT PUREE

Makes 12–16 ounces • Prep time: 5 minutes • Pressure time: 10 minutes

Although prunes are probably the most well-known food for mobilizing the digestive system, you have *lots* of fresh choices to help your baby's GI tract stay on track. Apricots are a deliciously sweet, high-fiber selection that can improve gut health. They're also packed with vitamins A and C and potassium. The dried form is easily found at your local market all year long.

1 cup dried apricots, no sugar added

1¾ cups water

1. Place the dried apricots and water into the multi-cooker, making sure the apricots are covered with water; secure the lid.

2. Cook on High Pressure for 10 minutes.

3. When the cook time is complete, turn off the multi-cooker. Let the steam release naturally for 10 minutes, then use the quick release valve to finish releasing the pressure.

4. After the float valve drops, remove the lid carefully.

5. With a slotted spoon, remove the apricots to a small bowl and let cool for 20 minutes. Save the water.

6. Add 1 cup of the reserved water to the apricots. Using an immersion blender, puree the mixture, adding more water as needed for the desired consistency.

7. Transfer the puree to a storage jar or container.

The Organic Advantage

When you choose organic dried fruit, you wisely avoid sulfur dioxide. This preservative may be used in conventional dried fruits to boost color and prolong shelf life, but it can also trigger asthmatic and allergic reactions. Another easy way to avoid sulfur dioxide: make your own dried fruit at home.

PEACH PUREE

Makes 16 ounces • Prep time: 5 minutes • Pressure time: 4 minutes

What's sweeter—the taste of a ripe, juicy peach or the smile on your baby's face taking in that first spoonful of peach puree? You can smile too, knowing that peaches provide your baby with vitamins A and C, potassium, and lutein. To expand the fruit horizons of your baby food repertoire, swap nectarines for the peaches in this recipe—no adjustments needed.

½ cup water

4 ripe peaches, halved and pitted

1. Place the water and then the peaches, skin side down, into the multi-cooker; secure the lid.

2. Cook on High Pressure for 4 minutes.

3. When the cook time is complete, turn off the multi-cooker. Use the quick release valve to release the pressure.

4. After the float valve drops, remove the lid carefully.

5. With a slotted spoon, remove the peaches to a small bowl and let cool for 20 minutes. Save the water.

6. Peel the peaches and return them to the bowl.

7. Add ¼ cup of the reserved water to the peaches. Using an immersion blender, puree the mixture, adding more water as needed for the desired consistency.

8. Transfer the puree to a storage jar or container.

{ PEACH PRIME TIME }

Peaches are definitely best in season. July and August are the best months to grab them at the market. Look for fragrant peaches that give slightly with a gentle squeeze. To quickly ripen firm peaches, place them in a paper bag with an apple at room temperature, poking holes in the bag in several places.

PLUM PUREE

Makes 12–16 ounces • Prep time: 5 minutes • Pressure time: 10 minutes

Even if your little one is not battling constipation, fiber-rich plum puree is a great way to keep things moving. But the nutrition benefits don't end there. Plums are impressively high in nutrients, containing more than fifteen vitamins and minerals. If your baby finds plums a tad on the tart side, mix this puree with yogurt or oatmeal once you've cleared the initial taste test.

1 cup dried plums, no sugar added	1¾ cups water

1. Place the dried plums and water into the multi-cooker, making sure the plums are covered with water; secure the lid.

2. Cook on High Pressure for 10 minutes.

3. When the cook time is complete, turn off the multi-cooker. Let the steam release naturally for 10 minutes, then use the quick release valve to finish releasing the pressure.

4. After the float valve drops, remove the lid carefully.

5. With a slotted spoon, remove the plums to a small bowl and let cool for 20 minutes. Save the water.

6. Add 1 cup of the reserved water to the plums. Using an immersion blender, puree the mixture, adding more water as needed for the desired consistency.

7. Transfer the puree to a storage jar or container.

{ HEALTHIER BAKING }

Plum puree is not just for babies! You can use it as a substitute for fat or oil in baked goods. Just skip the fat or oil in the recipe and swap in half as much plum puree. It blends best with chocolate. Hungry for brownies, anyone?

APPLE PUREE

Makes 28 ounces • Prep time: 10 minutes • Pressure time: 4 minutes

An apple a day may not keep the doctor *completely* away. After all, you need to keep up with those wellness checks! But it's still a super-healthy choice and classic fruit flavor to introduce into your baby's diet. Apple puree is a great way to enjoy all the benefits of apples, including vitamins and pectin—a type of fiber that feeds good bacteria in the gut. My favorite varieties to puree are Gala, Fuji, Jonagold, and Golden Delicious.

9 small apples, peeled, cored, and quartered

¼ cup water

1. Place the apples and water into the multi-cooker; secure the lid.

2. Cook on High Pressure for 4 minutes.

3. When the cook time is complete, turn off the multi-cooker. Let the steam release naturally for 5 minutes, then use the quick release valve to finish releasing the pressure.

4. After the float valve drops, remove the lid carefully.

5. With a slotted spoon, remove the apples to a medium bowl and let cool for 20 minutes. Save the water.

6. Place the apples into a blender jar or a food processor.

7. Blend until smooth, adding the reserved water as needed for the desired consistency.

8. Transfer the puree to a storage jar or container.

Pump Up the Pectin

Right now, your baby needs peeled apples. But when the time is right, leave that skin in place to get even more pectin. Beyond prebiotic benefits, pectin helps manage cholesterol levels, blood sugar levels, and weight. It's healthy to develop a taste for the peel as well as the juicy fruit!

GREEN BEAN PUREE

Makes 12 ounces • Prep time: 5 minutes • Pressure time: 4 minutes

High in vitamin A and rich in fiber, beans make a great green addition to your baby's diet. For now, they blend super easily into a smooth puree. You can adjust the consistency based on the stage your baby is in—leave the blend a little more textured when your baby is ready. Try adding a little basil too. As your baby's feeding menu expands, green beans are super finger foods as well.

1 cup water	4 cups green beans, trimmed

1. Place a steamer basket into the multi-cooker; add the water.

2. Add the green beans; secure the lid.

3. Cook on High Pressure for 4 minutes.

4. When the cook time is complete, turn off the multi-cooker. Let the steam release naturally for 10 minutes, then use the quick release valve to finish releasing the pressure.

5. After the float valve drops, remove the lid carefully.

6. With a slotted spoon, remove the green beans to a medium bowl and let cool for 20 minutes. Save the water.

7. Add ½ cup of the reserved water to the green beans. Using an immersion blender, puree the mixture, adding more water as needed for the desired consistency.

8. Transfer the puree to a storage jar or container.

{ FREEZE THE JUDGMENT }

Fresh is best . . . when it's truly fresh. But fresh green beans may be difficult to find at certain times of the year. Substitute frozen green beans instead of resorting to fresh beans with discoloration and squishy spots. Skip the canned varieties of veggies and fruits, which often contain added salt and sugar.

SPINACH PUREE

Makes 16 ounces • Prep time: 1 minute • Pressure time: 2 minutes

Spinach is a superfood for our bodies—both growing and grown, no matter our age. It packs high amounts of carotenoids, vitamin C, folic acid, iron, and calcium. It's also one of the top sources for vitamin K—important for strong bones. Although it's a delicate veggie to cook, using your multi-cooker makes it easy. You can whip up this puree with just 3 minutes of prep and pressure time!

---

4 cups prewashed
fresh spinach

½ cup water

---

1. Place the spinach and water into the multi-cooker; secure the lid.
2. Cook on High Pressure for 2 minutes.
3. When the cook time is complete, turn off the multi-cooker. Let the steam release naturally for 10 minutes, then use the quick release valve to finish releasing the pressure.
4. After the float valve drops, remove the lid carefully.
5. With a slotted spoon, remove the spinach to a medium bowl and let cool for 20 minutes. Save the water.
6. Using an immersion blender, puree the mixture, adding the reserved water as needed for the desired consistency. (You can also substitute breast milk or formula for a creamier consistency.)
7. Transfer the puree to a storage jar or container.

{ A VERY VERSATILE VEGGIE }

When your baby is ready for combination purees, spinach mixes well with apple and zucchini. As your baby grows into chunkier foods, try mixing this simple spinach puree with added herbs of your choice into creamy risotto. The whole family will love it—one meal and done!

CARROT PUREE

Makes 16–24 ounces • Prep time: 5 minutes • Pressure time: 4 minutes

It's no wonder carrots are often one of baby's first foods. Your baby will love them because they are just a bit sweet and easy to digest. You'll appreciate them because they are packed with nutrients such as vitamins A and C and calcium. Steaming carrots preserves the nutrients best, so your baby gets the maximum benefit. Ready for a little spice? Nutmeg is a perfect complement!

8 fresh carrots, peeled and cut into 2-inch pieces

1 cup water

1. Place the carrots and water into the multi-cooker; secure the lid.

2. Cook on High Pressure for 4 minutes.

3. When the cook time is complete, turn off the multi-cooker. Let the steam release naturally for 5 minutes, then use the quick release valve to finish releasing the pressure.

4. After the float valve drops, remove the lid carefully.

5. With a slotted spoon, remove the carrots to a medium bowl and let cool for 20 minutes. Save the water.

6. Using an immersion blender, puree the mixture, adding the reserved water as needed for the desired consistency.

7. Transfer the puree to a storage jar or container.

{ ## BALDING CARROTS ARE BETTER }

Look for carrots with minimal sprouting on top and fewer little "hairs" growing all along the vegetable. These are signs of growth—and that the carrot has been sitting around for a while. Fresher is better for flavor and nutrition!

PUMPKIN PUREE

Makes 16 ounces • Prep time: 10 minutes • Pressure time: 15 minutes

Introduce your baby to the taste of fall—and feel free to swipe a spoonful for yourself! This puree's naturally sweet flavor and smooth texture are reminiscent of indulging in pumpkin pie. And it's just as nutritious as it is delicious, with antioxidants, fiber, and potassium. It's also one of the best sources of beta-carotene. Add a sprinkle of cinnamon and nutmeg as your baby grows.

1½ cups water

1 (3- to 4-pound) sugar pumpkin or pie pumpkin, peeled, seeded, and cut into 1-inch cubes

1. Place the trivet into the multi-cooker; add the water.

2. Place the pumpkin cubes on the trivet; secure the lid.

3. Cook on High Pressure for 15 minutes.

4. When the cook time is complete, turn off the multi-cooker. Let the steam release naturally for 5 minutes, then use the quick release valve to finish releasing the pressure.

5. After the float valve drops, remove the lid carefully.

6. Test the pumpkin's tenderness with a fork. Cook longer in increments of 5 minutes, repeating the tenderness test and additional steaming as needed.

7. With a slotted spoon, remove the pumpkin cubes to a medium bowl and let cool for 20 minutes. Save the water.

8. Place the pumpkin into a blender jar or a food processor.

9. Add ½ to ¾ cup of the reserved water to the pumpkin. Blend the mixture, adding more water as needed for the desired consistency.

10. Transfer the puree to a storage jar or container.

{ SWEET FOR YOUR BUDGET }

When in season, pumpkin puree is very budget-friendly—make multiple batches to freeze and enjoy throughout the year. Beyond being a super baby food, pumpkin puree mixes well into soups, stews, and chilis for a boost of nutrients.

ZUCCHINI PUREE

Makes 20 ounces • Prep time: 5 minutes • Pressure time: 4 minutes

Nourish your baby's growing bones, skin, and teeth with the powerful nutrients in zucchini. Because this recipe takes so little time to prep and make in your multi-cooker, it's a great puree to stock over the summer months when zucchini is plentiful and full of ripe nutrition. Freeze it to enjoy throughout the year—you'll have a taste of summer ready anytime for you and your baby.

3 zucchini, cut into 1-inch chunks

1½ cups water

1. Place the zucchini and water into the multi-cooker; secure the lid.

2. Cook on High Pressure for 4 minutes.

3. When the cook time is complete, turn off the multi-cooker. Let the steam release naturally for 10 minutes, then use the quick release valve to finish releasing the pressure.

4. After the float valve drops, remove the lid carefully.

5. With a slotted spoon, remove the zucchini to a medium bowl and let cool for 20 minutes. Save the water.

6. Using an immersion blender, puree the mixture, adding the reserved water as needed for the desired consistency.

7. Transfer the puree to a storage jar or container.

{ ## TRY A TO Z }

Apples, peas, carrots . . . classic baby food flavors are great, but don't stop there. Research shows that children develop preferences very early. The more flavors of fruits and veggies they try (safely, one at a time) early in life, the more they may develop a fondness for those healthy tastes.

PEA PUREE

Makes 16 ounces • Prep time: 2 minutes • Pressure time: 4 minutes

Along with calcium, vitamins A and C, and iron, one cup of peas contains more protein than a tablespoon of peanut butter! Brightly colored peas make a great puree for baby and a wonderful little finger food as well. Because peas have a very small window of fresh availability in stores, frozen is the most convenient route to include them in your baby's diet.

---

12 ounces frozen peas   1 cup water

---

1. Place the peas and water into the multi-cooker; secure the lid.

2. Cook on High Pressure for 4 minutes.

3. When the cook time is complete, turn off the multi-cooker. Let the steam release naturally for 10 minutes, then use the quick release valve to finish releasing the pressure.

4. After the float valve drops, remove the lid carefully.

5. With a slotted spoon, remove the peas to a medium bowl and let cool for 20 minutes. Save the water.

6. Using an immersion blender, puree the mixture, adding the reserved water as needed for the desired consistency.

7. Transfer the puree to a storage jar or container.

{ PEAS, PLEASE }

You'll enjoy a more sophisticated taste of peas made just for you by adding a squeeze of lemon juice along with a few fresh mint leaves to the basic puree recipe above. Just make the additions to the portion you'll enjoy and pulse a few extra times to blend. It's delicious served with fish!

BELL PEPPER PUREE

Makes 24 ounces • Prep time: 5 minutes • Pressure time: 3 minutes

The bright colors of yellow, orange, and red bell peppers are markers of the nutrients they hold inside—called carotenoids. They serve up vitamins A and C, potassium, fiber, and folate in festive form. Although green peppers are nutritious, they tend to be more on the bitter side. In the early stages of your baby's feeding, stick with the warm colors for a sweet puree. You can even make a combo of all three.

---

2 bell peppers, cored, seeded, and thinly sliced

½ cup water

---

1. Place the peppers and water into the multi-cooker; secure the lid.
2. Cook on High Pressure for 3 minutes.
3. When the cook time is complete, turn off the multi-cooker. Use the quick release valve to release the pressure.
4. After the float valve drops, remove the lid carefully.
5. With a slotted spoon, remove the peppers to a medium bowl and cover with plastic wrap. Let steam for 10 minutes. Save the water.
6. Uncover the peppers and let cool for 10 minutes.
7. Using an immersion blender, puree the mixture, adding the reserved water as needed for the desired consistency.
8. Transfer the puree to a storage jar or container.

{ SEEING RED }

Although this puree isn't a flavor typically seen on store shelves, it's a slightly sweet treat for baby. Add it to yogurt for a creamy puree, or serve it on top of potatoes, rice, or chicken as your baby grows. Red pepper puree also makes a great addition to smoothies for the whole family!

CUCUMBER PUREE

Makes 12 ounces • Prep time: 5 minutes • Pressure time: 5 minutes

It may surprise you how this simple veggie can make a very refreshing puree, even when cooked! It's recommended that you wait until your baby is twelve months old before offering raw cucumber, but a quick steaming in your multi-cooker allows you to whip up a smooth, hydrating puree full of minerals like calcium and potassium.

1 English cucumber, trimmed and sliced into 1-inch rounds

½ cup water

1. Place the cucumber and water into the multi-cooker; secure the lid.

2. Cook on High Pressure for 5 minutes.

3. When the cook time is complete, turn off the multi-cooker. Use the quick release valve to release the pressure.

4. After the float valve drops, remove the lid carefull. Let cool for 10 minutes.

5. Transfer the cucumber and liquid to a blender jar; blend until smooth.

6. Transfer the puree to a storage jar or container.

MIX IN MORE NUTRITION

Cucumbers are refreshing but mostly water. Once you know that they sit well with your baby, you can mix them with other fruits and vegetables for greater nutritional benefit. Good partners: apple, pear, greens beans, avocado, and zucchini.

PEAR PUREE

Makes 24–32 ounces • Prep time: 10 minutes • Pressure time: 4 minutes

Great for digestive health, pears make an excellent stage 1 food for babies. The fruit offers a gently sweet taste along with fiber and vitamins A and C. Another benefit: the flavor of pears blends well with other fruits and vegetables when your baby is ready to explore combinations. Try different varieties of pears to see which you and your baby like best.

5 large pears, peeled, cored, and quartered

½ cup water

1. Place the pears and water into the multi-cooker; secure the lid.

2. Cook on High Pressure for 4 minutes.

3. When the cook time is complete, turn off the multi-cooker. Let the steam release naturally for 5 minutes, then use the quick release valve to finish releasing the pressure.

4. After the float valve drops, remove the lid carefully.

5. With a slotted spoon, remove the pears to a medium bowl and let cool for 20 minutes. Save the water.

6. Using an immersion blender, puree the mixture, adding the reserved water as needed for the desired consistency.

7. Transfer the puree to a storage jar or container.

Not Just for Babies

You can serve pear puree just like you would applesauce. Try spicing it with cinnamon or ginger. When your baby is ready, and for the rest of the family now, try mixing pear puree with plain Greek yogurt, oatmeal, even rice. For a special treat, top vanilla ice cream with pear puree.

BROCCOLI PUREE

Makes 20 ounces • Prep time: 2 minutes • Pressure time: 3 minutes

Broccoli is high in vitamins A and K and very satisfying. But what makes it so filling is lots of fiber, so it may be worth waiting to introduce this veggie until eight to ten months old. By that time, your baby's digestive tract should be able to handle it more easily and absorb all the goodness with less gas. As your little one grows into toddler food, they will love steamed little "trees."

5 cups broccoli florets   ¾ cup water

1. Place the broccoli and water into the multi-cooker; secure the lid.
2. Cook on High Pressure for 3 minutes.
3. When the cook time is complete, turn off the multi-cooker. Let the steam release naturally for 10 minutes, then use the quick release valve to finish releasing the pressure.
4. After the float valve drops, remove the lid carefully.
5. With a slotted spoon, remove the broccoli to a medium bowl and let cool for 20 minutes. Save the water.
6. Using an immersion blender, puree the mixture, adding the reserved water as needed for the desired consistency.
7. Transfer the puree to a storage jar or container.

{ NATURAL GAS REMEDY }

Ginger is an amazing digestive aid. Try putting a piece of raw, peeled ginger into the multi-cooker along with the broccoli. Or add a little grated ginger or ginger powder to the puree. Just remember to treat it as a new food and introduce it with a food that's already familiar.

BUTTERNUT SQUASH PUREE

Makes 40–48 ounces • Prep time: 5 minutes • Pressure time: 5 minutes

Butternut squash has a sweet and slightly nutty flavor that most babies find tasty. It will quickly become a favorite! And that's great news, because butternut squash is high in antioxidants and a good source of vitamins A and B6. One butternut squash makes *a lot* of baby food—another advantage to making it a regular in your baby food repertoire.

1 cup water

1 butternut squash, peeled, seeded and cut into 1-inch cubes

1. Place the trivet into the multi-cooker; add the water.

2. Place the squash on the trivet; secure the lid.

3. Cook on High Pressure for 5 minutes.

4. When the cook time is complete, turn off the multi-cooker. Let the steam release naturally for 10 minutes, then use the quick release valve to finish releasing the pressure.

5. After the float valve drops, remove the lid carefully.

6. With a slotted spoon, remove the squash to a large bowl and let cool for 10 minutes. Save the water.

7. Place the squash into a blender jar or a food processor.

8. Add ½ cup of the reserved water to the squash. Blend the mixture, adding more water as needed for the desired consistency.

9. Transfer the puree to a storage jar or container.

{ TACKLE THAT SQUASH }

To make the squash easier to handle, peel it first, then cut off a ¼-inch slice from the bottom and then a ¼-inch slice from below the stem. With the squash standing upright and stable, make one long cut down the middle. Use a metal spoon to scrape out the seeds. Cut the squash into slices, then work toward cubes.

CAULIFLOWER PUREE

Makes 20 ounces • Prep time: 2 minutes • Pressure time: 3 minutes

Despite its basic white exterior, this vegetable has a lot going for it! It's easy to find all year long and steams up very quickly. Cauliflower is loaded with vitamin C and fiber and offers a good amount of B vitamins, vitamin K, and choline—a nutrient important for memory and learning. Wait to introduce cauliflower until about eight months of age because it can cause gas in a developing tummy.

4 cups cauliflower florets

¾ cup water

1. Place the cauliflower and water into the multi-cooker; secure the lid.

2. Cook on High Pressure for 3 minutes.

3. When the cook time is complete, turn off the multi-cooker. Let the steam release naturally for 10 minutes, then use the quick release valve to finish releasing the pressure.

4. After the float valve drops, remove the lid carefully.

5. With a slotted spoon, remove the cauliflower to a medium bowl and let cool for 20 minutes. Save the water.

6. Using an immersion blender, puree the mixture, adding the reserved water as needed for the desired consistency.

7. Transfer the puree to a storage jar or container.

MOVE UP TO RICE

When your baby moves beyond purees, try cauliflower rice. It makes a great side dish or toddler meal. Simply pulse florets into rice-size pieces in a food processor. Then simmer in water until tender. Drain in a fine-mesh strainer, pressing with a spoon to release as much water as possible.

3-IN-1-POT PUREE

Makes 24 ounces • Prep time: 3 minutes • Pressure time: 6 minutes

Want to cook up a variety of single-ingredient purees but don't have much time? This 3-in-1-pot trick works wonders! Your baby can enjoy three different purees that come together in one small time frame. Another advantage beyond time savings: smaller batches make it easy to taste-test new foods. If your baby is under seven months old, peel the apples for gentler digestion.

1 cup water	1 cup baby carrots	1 medium apple, cored and cut into 1-inch cubes
1 cup frozen peas		

1. Place the trivet into the multi-cooker; add the water.

2. Fill each of three 12.5-ounce wide-mouth mason jars with one of the ingredients.

3. Place the uncovered jars on the trivet; secure the lid.

4. Cook on High Pressure for 6 minutes.

5. When the cook time is complete, turn off the multi-cooker. Let the steam release naturally for 5 minutes, then use the quick release valve to finish releasing the pressure.

6. After the float valve drops, remove the lid carefully.

7. Remove the jars from the multi-cooker and let cool for 20 minutes. Save the water.

8. Transfer the contents of each jar to separate small bowls.

9. Using an immersion blender, puree the mixtures, adding the reserved water as needed for the desired consistency.

10. Transfer the purees to storage jars or containers.

{ EXPLORE NEW TASTES }

Once you get the hang of this 3-in-1 multi-cooker method with the ingredients in the above recipe, go ahead and mix it up! Swap in different fruits and vegetables as long as they have similar cooking times. It makes it so easy to whip up a variety of single-ingredient flavors.

WHITE BEAN PUREE

Makes 40 ounces • Prep time: 1 minute • Pressure time: 28 minutes

White beans are a powerhouse of nutrients, including fiber and protein, and a good source of numerous micronutrients, including folate, magnesium, and vitamin B6. A great time to introduce beans into a baby's diet is between eight and ten months of age, to allow time for your little one's digestive system to develop—legumes can be a source of gassiness. With the ease of a multi-cooker, cooking beans is easy to fit into your schedule. There is no need for soaking overnight. Just pop the dried beans into your appliance and add water. You'll be ready to puree in no time!

2 cups dried white beans, rinsed

8 cups water

1. Place the beans and water into the multi-cooker, making sure the beans are covered by at least 1 inch of water; add more water as needed. Secure the lid.

2. Cook on High Pressure for 28 minutes.

3. When the cook time is complete, turn off the multi-cooker. Let the steam release naturally for 20 minutes, then use the quick release valve to finish releasing the pressure.

4. After the float valve drops, remove the lid carefully.

5. Drain the beans in a colander and let cool for 20 minutes.

6. Transfer the beans to a blender jar or a food processor.

7. Puree the beans, adding water as needed for the desired consistency.

8. Transfer the puree to a storage jar or container.

So Many Options

Every time you make a batch of white bean puree for baby food, keep a little to the side for homemade hummus; just add some herbs and oil.

BEET PUREE

Makes 16 ounces • Prep time: 5 minutes • Pressure time: 15 minutes

Beets are colorful packages of antioxidants as well as fiber, calcium, potassium, and vitamin C. When shopping for fresh beets to use in baby food, know that bigger is not better. Medium beets are much more tender and flavorful than large beets. For the best results, aim for beets around 1½ inches in diameter.

---

6 medium beets, trimmed, peeled, and cut into 1-inch cubes

1 cup water

---

1. Place the beets and water into the multi-cooker; secure the lid.

2. Cook on High Pressure for 15 minutes.

3. When the cook time is complete, turn off the multi-cooker. Let the steam release naturally for 10 minutes, then use the quick release valve to finish releasing the pressure.

4. After the float valve drops, remove the lid carefully.

5. With a slotted spoon, remove the beets to a medium bowl and let cool for 20 minutes. Discard the water.

6. Using an immersion blender, puree the mixture, adding fresh water as needed for the desired consistency.

7. Transfer the puree to a storage jar or container.

{ ## COLOR CHOICES }

Don't worry if you find a little red tint left on the spoon or in your baby's diaper after eating beets. The red pigment found in beets is natural. If the color staining bothers you, try golden or white beets instead.

OVERNIGHT YOGURT

Makes 40–48 ounces • Prep time: 5 minutes • Cook time: 24 hours

This yogurt is multi-cooker magic! With some preplanning you can get homemade results overnight with very little prep time. Babies love the taste and creamy texture of yogurt, so chances are you'll be going through a lot of it. And that's a good thing because you'll be giving your baby important probiotics for a healthy belly and a strong immune system.

2 quarts whole milk	10 grams probiotic yogurt starter

1. Pour the milk into the multi-cooker pot; secure the lid.

2. Press "Yogurt," then hold "Adjust" until it shows "Boil." (This will automatically heat the milk until it's the right temperature.)

3. When the multi-cooker indicates the milk is heated, press "Yogurt," then hold "Adjust" again to keep the temperature at 180ºF for 5 minutes. (This helps the yogurt thicken.)

4. Remove the pot from the multi-cooker and set aside to cool. Using a thermometer, make sure the milk is at 115ºF before moving to the next step.

5. Transfer 1 cup of milk from the pot to a small bowl; stir in the yogurt starter.

6. Pour the starter mixture back into the pot.

7. Return the pot to the multi-cooker; secure the lid.

8. Press "Yogurt," then "Adjust" to 24 hours.

9. When the cook time is complete, transfer the yogurt to a glass container and chill in the refrigerator.

{ ## WHOLESOME INGREDIENT }

Although it's recommended to wait until one year to introduce cow's milk to babies, yogurt containing milk is fine to start earlier. Using whole milk in this recipe makes it creamy and provides essential fats that growing babies need.

EGGPLANT PUREE

Makes 16 ounces • Prep time: 5 minutes • Pressure time: 3 minutes

Give your baby a boost of gut-healthy fiber with eggplant puree. It's also loaded with bone-boosting nutrients vitamin K and calcium for babies on the go! If your little one doesn't love the taste of eggplant puree on its own, don't give up on eggplant entirely. Once you cross the initial test, eggplant puree mixes well with apple to add a touch of sweetness.

1 medium eggplant, cut into 1-inch chunks

½ cup water

1. Place the eggplant and water into the multi-cooker; secure the lid.

2. Cook on High Pressure for 3 minutes.

3. When the cook time is complete, turn off the multi-cooker. Let the steam release naturally for 10 minutes, then use the quick release valve to finish releasing the pressure.

4. After the float valve drops, remove the lid carefully.

5. With a slotted spoon, remove the eggplant to a medium bowl and let cool for 20 minutes. Save the water.

6. Using an immersion blender, puree the mixture, adding the reserved water as needed for the desired consistency.

7. Transfer the puree to a storage jar or container.

THE PURPLE WONDER

While you're preparing baby food with a rainbow of natural colors, share the experience with your child. Let them see each fruit or vegetable as you say its name and color. Younger babies may not connect fully with the information until much later, but they'll enjoy the "conversation."

ASPARAGUS PUREE

Makes 16 ounces • Prep time: 5 minutes • Pressure time: 4 minutes

Asparagus makes such a great finger food for older babies. But you don't need to wait until that stage to start introducing this veggie, which is packed with vitamin C, iron, and protein (surprise!). Simply blend it into a puree. You'll want to wait to introduce asparagus—along with broccoli and cauliflower—until about eight months of age because it can sometimes cause gas in a developing tummy.

1 bunch asparagus, trimmed and cut into 1-inch pieces	½ cup water

1. Place the asparagus and water into the multi-cooker; secure the lid.

2. Cook on High Pressure for 4 minutes.

3. When the cook time is complete, turn off the multi-cooker. Let the steam release naturally for 10 minutes, then use the quick release valve to finish releasing the pressure.

4. After the float valve drops, remove the lid carefully.

5. With a slotted spoon, remove the asparagus to a small bowl and let cool for 20 minutes. Save the water.

6. Using an immersion blender, puree the mixture, adding the reserved water as needed for the desired consistency.

7. Transfer the puree to a storage jar or container.

{ ## WHAT'S THAT SMELL? }

After eating asparagus, your baby's urine may smell strange and even turn green. Don't worry: this is a harmless development brought on by the production of certain natural compounds as the asparagus is digested. It can happen to anyone, baby or grown-up.

RICE CEREAL

Makes 12 ounces • Prep time: 5 minutes • Pressure time: 4 minutes

Rice cereal has long been a first food for babies. And with good reason: it's mild-flavored, gentle on little tummies, and a great base to mix with lots of other purees when your baby is ready to expand their palate. To give homemade rice cereal a boost of iron, add a bit of formula or breast milk. You can swap in brown rice; just adjust the pressure time to 22 minutes.

½ cup white rice   1⅔ cups water, divided

1. Place the trivet into the multi-cooker; add 1 cup of the water.

2. In a 7-inch cake pan, combine the rice and remaining ⅔ cup water.

3. Using a sling, place the pan on the trivet; secure the lid.

4. Cook on High Pressure for 4 minutes.

5. When the cook time is complete, turn off the multi-cooker. Let the steam release naturally for 7 minutes, then use the quick release valve to finish releasing the pressure.

6. After the float valve drops, remove the lid carefully.

7. Remove the cake pan from the multi-cooker and let cool for 20 minutes.

8. Using an immersion blender, pulse the mixture, adding water, breast milk, or formula as needed for the desired consistency.

9. Transfer the cereal to a storage jar or container.

The Scoop on Rice

Some experts recommend moderating your rice consumption to limit your intake of arsenic, which the rice plant and grain tend to absorb more readily than other food crops do. Check with your pediatrician for recommendations on how often to serve it, balancing the nutrition benefits with any concerns.

OATMEAL PUREE

Makes 28 ounces • Prep time: 1 minute • Pressure time: 3 minutes

Oatmeal is a good way to add fiber to your little one's diet and help with digestion. It's very simple to make, and you can easily cook enough to feed the entire family; just blend only the portion you want for baby. Because not all oatmeal is gluten free (due to cross contamination), check oat labels. For those first bites, it may be necessary to add a bit of water, breast milk or formula to thin. For you now or for baby once you've checked for an allergy, sprinkle on a little cinnamon.

2 cups old fashioned oats	3½ cups water

1. Pour the oats into the multi-cooker, then add the water; secure the lid.

2. Cook on High Pressure for 3 minutes.

3. When the cook time is complete, turn off the multi-cooker. Let the steam release naturally for 10 minutes, then use the quick release valve to finish releasing the pressure.

4. After the float valve drops, remove the lid carefully. Let cool for 10 minutes.

5. Using an immersion blender, puree the mixture, adding water, breast milk, or formula as needed for the desired consistency.

6. Transfer the puree to a storage jar or container.

Now That's Better!

Once you start making homemade baby foods, you quickly discover how simple and inexpensive it is. But even more important, fresh is best for flavor. New eaters will be enticed to try all kinds of new foods much more easily when the food tastes good.

NO-COOK PUREES

While your multi-cooker makes quick work of preparing baby food, it's good to know some delicious no-cook purees that are also a breeze to prepare at home and great to take with you on the go. For these purees, simply wash and chop the fruit or vegetable and either mash it with a fork to eat right away or blend it with a bit of water for a smoother puree you can store and add to your freezer rotation.

AVOCADO PUREE

Avocado is such an easy first food, because it requires no cooking but delivers a creamy, mild flavor that most babies enjoy. Plus, the fruit is loaded with healthy fats and vitamins A and C.

- Serve ¼ avocado mashed with a fork.
- To create a baby food that can be frozen and stored, add 3 avocados to a blender with 2 tablespoons water and puree.

BANANA PUREE

Babies love bananas, and even big kids eat them up like crazy! Along with being a crowd-pleaser, bananas are high in potassium and vitamin C.

- Simply mash ½ banana with a fork for a single serving.
- Add a full banana with 1 teaspoon of water to a blender to create a smooth, blended baby food that can be stored and frozen.

MELON PUREE

With such a sweet flavor and high concentration of water, cantaloupe or any kind of melon makes a fun, refreshing treat with no need for cooking!

• Cut a ripe melon in half and scoop out the seeds. Remove the rind and dice into chunks. Mash or puree in a blender to serve.

• Adding a little banana or yogurt will give this puree a creamier texture, if you like.

• Melon in puree form doesn't freeze well for storage. You can, however, freeze it in cubes to puree when needed. Small cubes also make soothing treats in a baby-safe feeder or for babies ready for finger food.

PINEAPPLE PUREE

This no-cook puree is a tropical delight. The whole family will devour it, and it's full of vibrant flavor and vitamin C.

• When your baby is ready, mix in a little full-fat canned coconut milk.

• You can use frozen pineapple as well; just thaw before blending.

• Blend chopped pineapple in a blender until smooth, adding a little liquid if needed. Serve or freeze.

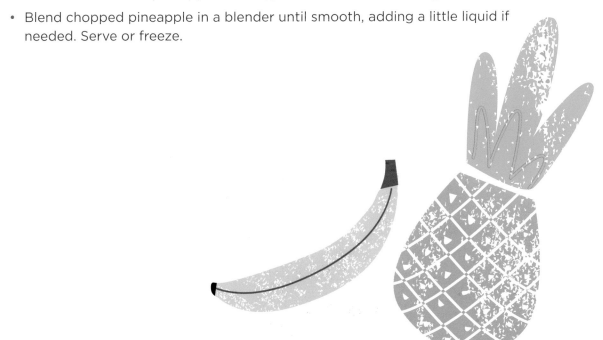

CREAMY COMBINATION PUREES

PUREE MIX AND MATCH

Stage 2 is a fun time to mix and match single-ingredient purees and play with new flavor combinations. When the freezer is stocked with single-ingredient puree cubes, exploring different tastes is even easier! Just thaw a cube of each single-ingredient puree, then mix in a small bowl. Below are some of my family's favorite puree combinations:

- Apple + Apricot
- Apple + Carrot + Pumpkin
- Apple + Spinach
- Apple + Broccoli
- Apple + Mango + Beet
- Pear + Mango + Spinach
- Pear + Pea + Spinach
- Pear + Plum
- Pea + Carrot
- Sweet Potato + Apple + Bell Pepper
- Sweet Potato + Carrot + Chickpea

- Sweet Potato + Mango + Carrot
- Green Bean + Spinach + Pear
- Zucchini + Pear + Chickpea
- Peach + Pumpkin + Carrot
- Carrot + Cauliflower
- Carrot + Beet
- Pumpkin + Chickpea + Spinach + Broccoli
- Butternut Squash + Carrot + Chickpea
- Butternut Squash + Peach

APPLE + BANANA + CARROT PUREE

Makes 24 ounces • Prep time: 10 minutes • Pressure time: 4 minutes

This puree is a blend of classic fruit and vegetable flavors that most babies love. The banana adds a special sweet, creamy touch! Every spoonful will be packed with nutrients to keep little bellies happy and full.

1 cup water

3 small apples, peeled, cored, and quartered

4 carrots, peeled and chopped into 1-inch pieces

1 medium banana

1. Place the trivet into the multi-cooker; add the water.

2. Add the apples and carrots to a steamer basket.

3. Place the steamer basket on the trivet; secure the lid.

4. Cook on High Pressure for 4 minutes.

5. When the cook time is complete, turn off the multi-cooker. Let the steam release naturally for 20 minutes, then use the quick release valve to finish releasing the pressure.

6. After the float valve drops, remove the lid carefully.

7. Transfer the apples and carrots to a medium bowl and let cool for 20 minutes. Save the water.

8. Place the apples and carrots into a blender jar or a food processor.

9. Add ¼ cup of the reserved water and the banana. Blend the mixture, adding more water as needed for the desired consistency.

10. Transfer the puree to a storage jar or container.

APPLES TO APPLES

Deciding what kind of apple to include? My family likes Gala, Fuji, Jonagold, or Golden Delicious in this blend. Bonus: These fruit choices are easily available throughout the year.

APPLE-CINNAMON OATMEAL PUREE

Makes 24 ounces • Prep time: 5 minutes • Pressure time: 4 minutes

Your family will wake up easier when they catch the scent of apple-cinnamon oatmeal wafting from the kitchen. Blend up the portion you want for your little one, and keep some chunkier for the rest of the family, if you like. It's simple to adjust the texture and make everyone happy with this warm, comforting dish. Because not all oatmeal is gluten free (due to cross contamination), check oat labels. Excellent apple choices: Gala, Fuji, Jonagold, or Golden Delicious. Swap in some pear for another flavor option.

1 cup old fashioned oats 2½ cups water	3 small apples, peeled, cored, and quartered	1 teaspoon ground cinnamon

1. Pour the oats into the multi-cooker, then add the water.

2. Insert the trivet.

3. Add the apples to a steamer basket and place on top of the trivet; sprinkle the cinnamon on top. Secure the lid.

4. Cook on High Pressure for 4 minutes.

5. When the cook time is complete, turn off the multi-cooker. Let the steam release naturally for 10 minutes, then use the quick release valve to finish releasing the pressure.

6. After the float valve drops, remove the lid carefully.

7. Remove the steamer basket and let the apples cool for 5 minutes.

8. Add the apples to the multi-cooker and, using an immersion blender, puree the mixture.

9. Transfer the puree to a storage jar or container.

BLUEBERRY + APPLE + OATS PUREE

Makes 32 ounces • Prep time: 5 minutes • Pressure time: 4 minutes

Blueberries add a tart burst of antioxidants that jazz up the classic oatmeal flavor. Fresh is best, but frozen berries that are thawed can also work off-season. Tasty apples that work well: Gala, Fuji, Jonagold, or Golden Delicious. Because not all oatmeal is gluten free (due to cross contamination), check oat labels.

---

1 cup old fashioned oats

2½ cups water

3 small apples, peeled, cored, and quartered

1 cup blueberries

---

1. Pour the oatmeal into the multi-cooker, then add the water.

2. Insert the trivet.

3. Add the apples and blueberries to a steamer basket and place on top of the trivet; secure the lid.

4. Cook on High Pressure for 4 minutes.

5. When the cook time is complete, turn off the multi-cooker. Let the steam release naturally for 10 minutes, then use the quick release valve to finish releasing the pressure.

6. After the float valve drops, remove the lid carefully.

7. Remove the steamer basket and let the fruit cool for 5 minutes.

8. Add the fruit to the multi-cooker and, using an immersion blender, puree the mixture.

9. Transfer the puree to a storage jar or container.

{ ## BERRY TREASURE HUNT

If you have a berry patch near you, go berry picking as a family! It's a fun activity that helps little ones see how their fruit grows and appreciate it all the more. }

MIXED BERRY PUREE

Makes 8 ounces • Prep time: 1 minute • Pressure time: 3 minutes

Berries are great sources of antioxidants and such a taste treat for your little one, too. Use any mix of berries you want in this recipe. No matter which berries you choose, each will be a delicious and nutritious addition to your baby's diet. And don't worry if your baby's diaper color goes dark for a few days after eating color-rich berries, especially blueberries.

1 cup blueberries   ½ cup blackberries
½ cup raspberries   ¼ cup water

1. Place the berries and water into the multi-cooker; secure the lid.

2. Cook on High Pressure for 3 minutes.

3. When the cook time is complete, turn off the multi-cooker. Let the steam release naturally for 10 minutes, then use the quick release valve to finish releasing the pressure.

4. After the float valve drops, remove the lid carefully.

5. Transfer the berry mixture to a medium bowl and let cool for 10 minutes.

6. Using an immersion blender, puree the mixture.

7. Transfer the puree to a storage jar or container.

{ ## THICK AND THIN

Berry purees can be tricky to get to just the right thickness. If your result is too thin, try adding some apple for a thicker consistency. Or serve your berry puree on top of or mixed with plain Greek yogurt—it's a great breakfast for anyone in the family. }

MANGO + APPLE + KIWI PUREE

Makes 16 ounces • Prep time: 5 minutes • Pressure time: 4 minutes

Brighten up your baby's day and boost their vitamin C intake by adding a tropical twist to the usual apples. Vibrant mango and kiwi will make you want to taste this puree yourself! The best blending apple varieties: Gala, Fuji, Jonagold, or Golden Delicious.

---

1 cup water

3 small apples, peeled, cored, and quartered

1 kiwi, peeled and quartered

1 mango, peeled, pitted, and quartered

---

1. Place the trivet into the multi-cooker; add the water.

2. Add the apples, kiwi, and mango to a steamer basket.

3. Place the steamer basket on the trivet; secure the lid.

4. Cook on High Pressure for 4 minutes.

5. When the cook time is complete, turn off the multi-cooker. Let the steam release naturally for 5 minutes, then use the quick release valve to finish releasing the pressure.

6. After the float valve drops, remove the lid carefully.

7. Transfer the fruit to a medium bowl and let cool for 20 minutes. Save the water.

8. Place the fruit into a blender jar or a food processor.

9. Blend the mixture, adding the reserved water as needed for the desired consistency.

10. Transfer the puree to a storage jar or container.

Look Beyond Looks

For the best flavor, choose fresh kiwis and mangoes that are slightly soft to the touch but not squishy. Your touch test is a much better indicator than judging by appearance.

PEACH + APPLE + OATS PUREE

Makes 32 ounces • Prep time: 5 minutes • Pressure time: 4 minutes

Luscious peach gives you yet another option to try beyond your basic apple oatmeal. It's a simple addition that refreshes the flavor and adds digestive and immune-boosting benefits. Fresh is best, but frozen peaches that are thawed can also work off-season. Juicy apple varieties to try in this puree: Gala, Fuji, Jonagold, or Golden Delicious. Because not all oatmeal is gluten free (due to cross contamination), check oat labels.

1 cup old fashioned oats 2½ cups water	3 small peaches, peeled, halved, and pitted	3 small apples, peeled, cored, and quartered

1. Pour the oats into the multi-cooker, then add the water.
2. Insert the trivet.
3. Add the peaches and apples to a steamer basket and place on top of the trivet; secure the lid.
4. Cook on High Pressure for 4 minutes.
5. When the cook time is complete, turn off the multi-cooker. Let the steam release naturally for 10 minutes, then use the quick release valve to finish releasing the pressure.
6. After the float valve drops, remove the lid carefully.
7. Remove the steamer basket and let the fruit cool for 5 minutes.
8. Add the fruit to the multi-cooker and, using an immersion blender, puree the mixture.
9. Transfer the puree to a storage jar or container.

Easy-Peel Peaches

Here's a little kitchen trick: Bring a medium pot of water to a boil. Add the peaches and blanch for about 45 seconds. With a slotted spoon, remove the peaches and fully submerge in an ice bath. Peel the skin with your fingers or a sharp paring knife.

PEAR + SPINACH + GREEN BEAN PUREE

Makes 32 ounces • Prep time: 5 minutes • Pressure time: 4 minutes

Give your baby a taste for nutrient-packed greens right from the start! It's easy and delicious with this puree that's like a super green smoothie for your little one. The mild sweetness of the pear helps balance out the rest of the greens.

---

1 cup water

3 small pears, peeled, cored, and quartered

2 cups fresh spinach

2 cups green beans, trimmed

---

1. Place the trivet into the multi-cooker; add the water.

2. Add the pears, spinach, and green beans to a steamer basket and place on top of the trivet; secure the lid.

3. Cook on High Pressure for 4 minutes.

4. When the cook time is complete, turn off the multi-cooker. Let the steam release naturally for 10 minutes, then use the quick release valve to finish releasing the pressure.

5. After the float valve drops, remove the lid carefully.

6. Remove the steamer basket and let the mixture cool for 5 minutes.

7. Transfer the mixture to a blender jar or a food processor and puree.

8. Transfer the puree to a storage jar or container.

{ ## SMOOTH SPINACH }

Fresh spinach can be gritty. After removing the stems, soak it in cold water for 2 minutes. Rinse thoroughly under cool running water and pat dry with paper towels. Even "prewashed" should get a rinse.

PEAR + BANANA PUREE

Makes 16 ounces • Prep time: 5 minutes • Pressure time: 4 minutes

Pear is a favorite ingredient for baby food purees at all stages. That's because the fruit is mildly sweet, simple to blend with other flavors, easy to digest, and packed with fiber and vitamins A and C. Just one perfect pairing for pear: sweet, creamy, mashed banana.

---

1 cup water

2 large pears, peel on, cored and quartered

1 medium banana

---

1. Place the trivet into the multi-cooker; add the water.

2. Add the pears to a steamer basket and place on top of the trivet; secure the lid.

3. Cook on High Pressure for 4 minutes.

4. When the cook time is complete, turn off the multi-cooker. Let the steam release naturally for 5 minutes, then use the quick release valve to finish releasing the pressure.

5. After the float valve drops, remove the lid carefully.

6. Remove the steamer basket and let the pears cool for 20 minutes. Save the water.

7. Transfer the mixture to a blender jar or a food processor. Add the banana and ¼ cup of the reserved water; puree the mixture adding more water as needed for the desired consistency.

8. Transfer the puree to a storage jar or container.

{ NOT JUST FOR APPLES }

Have an apple corer tool in your utensil drawer? Pull it out to use with pears too. Work from the fruit's base to remove the core.

PEAR + KALE + RICE PUREE

Makes 28 ounces • Prep time: 5 minutes • Pressure time: 4 minutes

Pear and kale is a popular gourmet salad combination. But why should littles ones miss out on experiencing the delicious flavor blend? Here's the beginning-eater version. Beyond great taste, this puree serves up protein in a way that's gentle on baby's tummy.

---

2 large pears, peel on, cored and quartered

½ cup loose kale leaves
1⅔ cups water, divided

½ cup rice

---

1. Place the pears, kale, and 1 cup of the water into the multi-cooker; insert the trivet.

2. Add the remaining ⅔ cup water to a 7-inch round cake pan; add the rice, making sure to submerge it.

3. Using a sling, lower the cake pan onto the trivet; secure the lid.

4. Cook on High Pressure for 4 minutes.

5. When the cook time is complete, turn off the multi-cooker. Let the steam release naturally for 5 minutes, then use the quick release valve to finish releasing the pressure.

6. After the float valve drops, remove the lid carefully.

7. Allow the contents to cool in the multi-cooker for 20 minutes.

8. Save the water. Transfer the rice and the pear-kale mixture to a blender jar or a food processor; puree the mixture, adding the reserved water as needed for the desired consistency.

9. Transfer the puree to a storage jar or container.

{ ## KALE AT YOUR FINGERTIPS }

If your family has the right space and environment, consider growing your own kale. It's great to have on hand for purees, salads, smoothies, and more. And it looks pretty in your garden!

PUMPKIN + BANANA + CHIA PUREE

Makes 16 ounces • Prep time: 10 minutes • Pressure time: 15 minutes

This puree is like a magnificent blend of two classic desserts: pumpkin pie and banana pudding. But with only natural sugars, it makes a nutritious meal for your baby—and yummy nutrition for whoever else sneaks a spoonful or two or three. The addition of ground chia seeds gives a boost of omega-3 fatty acids, antioxidants, fiber, iron, and calcium.

1½ cups water

1 (3- to 4-pound) sugar pumpkin or pie pumpkin, peeled, seeded, and cut into 1-inch cubes

1 banana

1½ teaspoons ground chia seeds

1. Place the trivet into the multi-cooker; add the water.

2. Place the pumpkin cubes on the trivet; secure the lid.

3. Cook on High Pressure for 15 minutes.

4. When the cook time is complete, turn off the multi-cooker. Let the steam release naturally for 5 minutes, then use the quick release valve to finish releasing the pressure.

5. After the float valve drops, remove the lid carefully.

6. Test the pumpkin's tenderness with a fork. Cook longer in increments of 5 minutes, repeating the tenderness test and additional steaming as needed.

7. With a slotted spoon, remove the pumpkin cubes to a medium bowl and let cool for 20 minutes. Save the water.

8. Place the pumpkin into a blender jar or a food processor. Add the banana and the chia seeds.

9. Blend the mixture, adding the reserved water as needed for the desired consistency.

10. Transfer the puree to a storage jar or container.

GINGERBREAD PEAR PUREE

Makes 16 ounces • Prep time: 5 minutes • Pressure time: 4 minutes

Sweet and spice and everything nice . . . this puree is sure to become one of your family's favorite flavor combinations. While there isn't actually any gingerbread in this puree, one taste (or even just the scent) will convince you that the recipe is named perfecly.

| 2 large Bartlett pears, peeled, halved, and cored | 1 ounce fresh gingerroot (about 2½-inch piece) | 1 cinnamon stick
½ cup water |

1. Place the pears, gingerroot, cinnamon stick, and water into the multi-cooker; secure the lid.
2. Cook on High Pressure for 4 minutes.
3. When the cook time is complete, turn off the multi-cooker. Use the quick release valve to release the pressure.
4. After the float valve drops, remove the lid carefully.
5. Allow the contents to cool in the multi-cooker for 20 minutes.
6. Discard the ginger and cinnamon stick.
7. Using an immersion blender, puree the mixture.
8. Transfer the puree to a storage jar or container.

GREAT GINGER!

Ginger has a long history of use as a tummy soother. It promotes healthy digestion and relieves gas. And it's so easy to add to purees, smoothies, and more!

PEAR + MANGO + SPINACH PUREE

Makes 28 ounces • Prep time: 5 minutes • Pressure time: 4 minutes

Combine superfood spinach with delightful mango and pears for just the right amount of sweetness. Your little one is sure to love the taste and texture, while you'll appreciate the good nutrition. Get inspired by the flavors to create your own version of this puree as a salad!

1 cup water

3 small pears, peeled, cored, and quartered

1 mango, peeled, halved, and pitted

1 cup fresh spinach

1. Place the trivet into the multi-cooker; add the water.

2. Add the pears, mango, and spinach to a steamer basket and place on top of the trivet; secure the lid.

3. Cook on High Pressure for 4 minutes.

4. When the cook time is complete, turn off the multi-cooker. Use the quick release valve to release the pressure.

5. After the float valve drops, remove the lid carefully.

6. Remove the steamer basket and let the mixture cool for 5 minutes. Save the water.

7. Transfer the mixture to a blender jar or a food processor. Add ¼ cup of the reserved water and puree, adding more water as needed for the desired consistency.

8. Transfer the puree to a storage jar or container.

{ ## MANGO MAGIC

Need to ripen a mango that's still a bit hard? Pop it into a brown paper bag to speed the process. }

SPINACH + PEAR + PEA PUREE

Makes 32 ounces • Prep time: 5 minutes • Pressure time: 4 minutes

Pear is a wonderful neutralizer in this green powerhouse puree, bringing harmony to the spinach and pea flavors. You can sneak in tons of nutrition without your baby turning up their nose. The bright green color makes it lots of fun to eat!

1 cup water

2 cups fresh spinach

3 small pears, peeled, cored, and quartered

12 ounces frozen peas

1. Place the trivet into the multi-cooker; add the water.

2. Add the spinach, pears, and peas to a steamer basket and place on top of the trivet; secure the lid.

3. Cook on High Pressure for 4 minutes.

4. When the cook time is complete, turn off the multi-cooker. Let the steam release naturally for 10 minutes, then use the quick release valve to finish releasing the pressure.

5. After the float valve drops, remove the lid carefully.

6. Remove the steamer basket and let the mixture cool for 5 minutes.

7. Transfer the mixture to a blender jar or a food processor. Puree the mixture.

8. Transfer the puree to a storage jar or container.

{ PICKING PEARS }

Because pears can be delicate, it's not a bad idea to choose ones that will ripen at home, rather than ones that are already ripe at the market.

APPLE + CORN + OATS PUREE

Makes 24 ounces • Prep time: 5 minutes • Pressure time: 3 minutes

If cornbread is a favorite in your family, try this puree. The blend of apples, corn, and oatmeal has the same hearty texture and a similar taste. So when the bread basket comes out, share this recipe with your baby to mimic what you're eating. Because not all oatmeal is gluten free (due to cross contamination), check oat labels.

---

1 cup old fashioned oats

1¾ cups water

2 small apples, peeled, cored, and quartered

1 cup whole kernel corn

---

1. Pour the oats into the multi-cooker, then add the water; insert the trivet.

2. Add the apples and corn to a steamer basket and place on top of the trivet; secure the lid.

3. Cook on High Pressure for 3 minutes.

4. When the cook time is complete, turn off the multi-cooker. Let the steam release naturally for 10 minutes, then use the quick release valve to finish releasing the pressure.

5. After the float valve drops, remove the lid carefully.

6. Remove the steamer basket and let the mixture cool for 5 minutes.

7. Remove the trivet.

8. Add the apples and corn to the multi-cooker and, using an immersion blender, puree the mixture.

9. Transfer the puree to a storage jar or container.

{ ## APPLE PICKING

When it comes to juicy apples to add to a multi-cooker recipe, my family turns to Gala, Fuji, Jonagold, and Golden Delicious. }

SQUASH + APPLE + CORN PUREE

Makes 56 ounces • Prep time: 10 minutes • Pressure time: 15 minutes

Butternut squash goes well with just about every other vegetable, and it's one that most babies take to quickly. Here we've paired it with apples and corn to create a sweet and slightly savory puree. Swap the butternut squash for yellow squash in the summer for sunshine in a bowl!

1 cup water	1 butternut squash, peeled, seeded and cut into 1-inch cubes	2 small apples, peeled, cored, and quartered
		1 cup whole kernel corn

1. Place a steamer basket into the multi-cooker; add the water.

2. Add the squash, apples, and corn; secure the lid.

3. Cook on High Pressure for 15 minutes.

4. When the cook time is complete, turn off the multi-cooker. Let the steam release naturally for 10 minutes, then use the quick release valve to finish releasing the pressure.

5. After the float valve drops, remove the lid carefully.

6. Remove the steamer basket and let the mixture cool for 10 minutes. Save the water.

7. Transfer the mixture to a blender jar or a food processor; puree, adding the reserved water as needed for the desired consistency.

8. Transfer the puree to a storage jar or container.

LONG LIVE SQUASH

Another benefit beyond the taste and nutrition: butternut squash will stay good for one to three months! So if life with your baby gets a little busy, keep a squash on hand—stored in a cool, dark place.

ZUCCHINI + BANANA PUREE

Makes 20 ounces • Prep time: 5 minutes • Pressure time: 4 minutes

Ahh, summers of zucchini plants growing like crazy and trying to make enough bread to keep up! When it's zucchini everything for a few months, enjoy some puree now and freeze some for later. There's sure to be plenty of zucchini left for that classic bread as well.

3 zucchini, cut into 1-inch chunks	½ cup water	1 banana

1. Place the zucchini and water into the multi-cooker; secure the lid.
2. Cook on High Pressure for 4 minutes.
3. When the cook time is complete, turn off the multi-cooker. Let the steam release naturally for 10 minutes, then use the quick release valve to finish releasing the pressure.
4. After the float valve drops, remove the lid carefully.
5. With a slotted spoon, remove the zucchini to a medium bowl and let cool for 20 minutes.
6. Add the banana to the bowl.
7. Using an immersion blender, puree the mixture.
8. Transfer the puree to a storage jar or container.

{ **"BREAD" FOR BABY** }

For a pureed version of that summer favorite, zucchini banana bread, mix Oatmeal Puree (page 55) with this puree recipe. If you're feeling adventurous, add a dash of cinnamon too.

SWEET POTATO + CORN PUREE

Makes 16 ounces • Prep time: 5 minutes • Pressure time: 15 minutes

Sweet potato and corn is a delicious blend in chowder and hash. So why not offer it as a baby food puree packed with rich, sweet taste—not to mention fiber, potassium, calcium, and vitamins A, C, and E? It's ready quickly, so you can enjoy more sweet tastes of life—like fresh air and family time.

1 cup water	1 sweet potato, peeled and cut into ¼-inch slices	1 cup whole kernel corn

1. Place a steamer basket into the multi-cooker; add the water.

2. Add the sweet potato and corn; secure the lid.

3. Cook on High Pressure for 15 minutes.

4. When the cook time is complete, turn off the multi-cooker. Let the steam release naturally for 10 minutes, then use the quick release valve to finish releasing the pressure.

5. After the float valve drops, remove the lid carefully.

6. Remove the steamer basket and let the mixture cool for 20 minutes. Save the water.

7. Transfer the mixture to a blender jar or a food processor; add ¼ cup of the reserved water. Puree, adding more water as needed for the desired consistency.

8. Transfer the puree to a storage jar or container.

{ ## PUREE ALL GROWN UP }

Always be on the lookout for smart ways to bring purees into table foods. They can add so much easy flavor and nutrition for the entire family! A perfect match for this puree: risotto.

STRAWBERRY APPLESAUCE

Makes 16 ounces • Prep time: 5 minutes • Pressure time: 5 minutes

While so many foods go great with apples, strawberries make an especially delicious, summery treat. This sweet puree is full of antioxidants as well as folate and potassium. Try Gala, Fuji, Jonagold, or Golden Delicious apples as juicy picks.

1 cup water	4 small apples, peeled, cored, and quartered	1 cup strawberries, stemmed and quartered

1. Place a steamer basket into the multi-cooker; add the water.

2. Add the apples; secure the lid.

3. Cook on High Pressure for 5 minutes.

4. When the cook time is complete, turn off the multi-cooker. Let the steam release naturally for 5 minutes, then use the quick release valve to finish releasing the pressure.

5. After the float valve drops, remove the lid carefully.

6. Remove the steamer basket and let the apples cool for 20 minutes. Save the water.

7. Transfer the mixture to a blender jar or a food processor; add the strawberries and ¼ cup of the reserved water. Puree, adding more water as needed for the desired consistency.

8. Transfer the puree to a storage jar or container.

WAIT UNTIL ONE

Due to allergy concerns, some pediatric experts recommend waiting until your baby is a year old to introduce strawberries—especially if your baby has other food sensitivities or a history of allergies.

SUPER GREEN PUREE

Makes 10 ounces • Prep time: 5 minutes • Pressure time: 5 minutes

Butter in baby food? You bet it's a healthy addition! Growing baby brains need lots of fats to feed their super-fast development. That's why this super puree is perfect baby fuel. And with *four* vegetables included, it introduces a little texture and a lot of nutrition in every bite.

1 tablespoon unsalted butter

1 cup fresh spinach

½ cup water

2 cups green beans, trimmed

1 bunch asparagus, trimmed

½ cup frozen shelled edamame

1. Add the butter to the multi-cooker; press Sauté and heat, uncovered, until the butter melts.

2. Add the spinach and sauté for 2 minutes until wilted and dark green.

3. Turn off the multi-cooker.

4. Add the water, then add the green beans, asparagus, and edamame; secure the lid.

5. Cook on High Pressure for 5 minutes.

6. When the cook time is complete, turn off the multi-cooker. Use the quick release valve to release the pressure.

7. After the float valve drops, remove the lid carefully.

8. Using an immersion blender, puree in the multi-cooker.

9. Transfer the puree to a storage jar or container.

NO EDAMAME?

Whether edamame isn't on hand or your baby eats soy-free, you can easily swap in frozen peas. Always look for ways to customize purees for your kitchen and your baby's tastes and needs.

SWEET POTATO + RED PEPPER + WHITE BEAN PUREE

Makes 24 ounces • Prep time: 5 minutes • Pressure time: 5 minutes

This blend offers all kinds of nutrients but is especially rich in iron and protein, making it a great meatless meal for your baby and also a smart addition to sauces or chili for the whole family. If you're out of red bell pepper, you can substitute orange or yellow.

1 sweet potato, peeled and cut into small chunks

1 red bell pepper, cored, seeded, and cut into small chunks

1 (15-ounce) can great Northern beans, drained and rinsed

1 cup water

1. Place the sweet potato, bell pepper, beans, and water into the multi-cooker; secure the lid.

2. Cook on High Pressure for 5 minutes.

3. When the cook time is complete, turn off the multi-cooker. Let the steam release naturally for 5 minutes, then use the quick release valve to finish releasing the pressure.

4. After the float valve drops, remove the lid carefully.

5. Let the mixture cool for 20 minutes.

6. Using an immersion blender, puree the mixture in the multi-cooker.

7. Transfer the puree to a storage jar or container.

{ ## PEPPER POSSIBILITIES }

Keeping fresh bell peppers on hand in your kitchen is a smart idea. Simple to prep, they make great additions to purees, salads, stir-fries, and more.

BEET PUREE + GREEK YOGURT

Makes 32 ounces • Prep time: 5 minutes • Pressure time: 15 minutes

Every pretty pink spoonful of this blend wil give your baby a powerful surge of vitamins and probiotics to boost tummy health. It's a great way to sneek in beets, since the creamy sweetness of the yogurt tempers the beets' strong flavor.

---

6 medium beets, stems cut off and cut into 1-inch cubes

1 cup water

2 cups plain Greek yogurt

---

1. Place the beets and water into the multi-cooker; secure the lid.

2. Cook on High Pressure for 15 minutes.

3. When the cook time is complete, turn off the multi-cooker. Let the steam release naturally for 10 minutes, then use the quick release valve to finish releasing the pressure.

4. After the float valve drops, remove the lid carefully.

5. With a slotted spoon, remove the beets to a medium bowl and let cool for 10 minutes.

6. Add the yogurt to the bowl.

7. Using an immersion blender, puree the mixture.

8. Transfer the puree to a storage jar or container.

{ DIY YOGURT }

Try making your own yogurt at home with the recipe on page 49—it's simple and saves money!

RED LENTIL + CARROT PUREE

Makes 16 ounces • Prep time: 5 minutes • Pressure time: 5 minutes

Lentils are related to peas and packed with protein. They take on the flavor of whatever they are mixed with, making them super-easy to use in purees for babies and sauces, soups, and stews for the rest of the family.

1 cup dried red lentils	1 carrot, peeled and cut into 2-inch pieces	2 cups water

1. Place the lentils, carrot, and water into the multi-cooker; secure the lid.

2. Cook on High Pressure for 5 minutes.

3. When the cook time is complete, turn off the multi-cooker. Let the steam release naturally for 5 minutes, then use the quick release valve to finish releasing the pressure.

4. After the float valve drops, remove the lid carefully.

5. With a slotted spoon, remove the mixture to a medium bowl and let cool for 20 minutes. Save the water.

6. Using an immersion blender, puree the mixture, adding the reserved water as needed for the desired consistency.

7. Transfer the puree to a storage jar or container.

{ ## MEATLESS FAMILY DINNER }

This nutritious blend can be a family meal as well as a baby puree. Double or triple the batch and only puree the serving size you need for baby. Leave the consistency thicker for everyone else and serve alongside bread and a salad.

CARROT + PARSNIP PUREE

Makes 20 ounces • Prep time: 5 minutes • Pressure time: 4 minutes

Fill your baby's bowl with some fabulous root vegetables. Easily available year round, carrots offer nutrients that support immunity and eye health. Parsnips are at their best in winter, serving up a nutty, sweet flavor along with calcium and vitamin C.

4 carrots, peeled and cut into 2-inch pieces	4 parsnips, peeled and cut into 2-inch pieces	1 cup water

1. Place the carrots, parsnips, and water into the multi-cooker; secure the lid.

2. Cook on High Pressure for 4 minutes.

3. When the cook time is complete, turn off the multi-cooker. Let the steam release naturally for 5 minutes, then use the quick release valve to finish releasing the pressure.

4. After the float valve drops, remove the lid carefully.

5. With a slotted spoon, remove the mixture to a medium bowl and let cool for 20 minutes. Save the water.

6. Transfer the mixture to a blender jar or a food processor; puree, adding the reserved water as needed for the desired consistency.

7. Transfer the puree to a storage jar or container.

PARSNIP SUBSTITUTES

No parsnips? Try subsitituting turnips or sweet potatoes for a similar taste. There are so many tasty root vegetables to explore with your baby!

PUREE ADD-INS

As a mom of six, I've discovered at least a few ways to make a meal more fun for all ages. At the top of the list: give the kids something to dip or mix in. (They feel like little food scientists!) Now, your baby can't quite choose their favorite mix-ins yet, but you can help them explore tastes and textures once you know that they can handle those single-ingredient purees and a few mixed purees as well. Below is a list of mix-ins that my family likes to have available to bring a greater depth of flavor and spice to those creamy little dishes.

HERBS AND SPICES are fun to play with in recipes; be sure to start with just a pinch added to your purees. There are so many flavor combinations you can create simply by adding a dash of cinnamon or a touch of mint. You don't want the results to be too spicy or overwhelming. Remember, these are your baby's first foods. Your little one hasn't developed a palate beyond formula or breast milk, so any food is a new taste for them.

- A few of our family favorites: cinnamon, nutmeg, basil, rosemary, oregano, cumin, turmeric, coriander, cardamom, allspice, and a squeeze of lemon or orange (or the zest).

YOGURT is one of the easiest additions to purees. It helps make them creamy and, at times, more palatable. You can add in any of your favorite plain yogurts (full-fat or Greek are great options), or even make your own with the recipe on page 49. It's best to avoid flavored options—they usually have a high sugar content.

- Start by adding a spoonful to any of your baby's purees; you can build up from there.

COTTAGE CHEESE is a great mix-in for purees, boosting both calcium and protein content. Much like yogurt, it adds creamy texture and flavor. Cottage cheese is a good option for chunky purees, starting with stage 3.

• Other cheeses can work as well; just finely grate before adding to purees.

OATMEAL is a great mix-in for adding fiber and thickening purees. You can also mix it simply with formula or breast milk to create a "cereal" for baby.

• Other grains will work as well. Just run the dry oats or grains through the food processor or pulse in the blender to create a powder or flour-like consistency and start mixing.

STAGE 3

CHUNKY COMBINATION PUREES

APPLE-CHICKEN RICE

Makes 28 ounces • Prep time: 5 minutes • Pressure time: 10 minutes

If your baby is eating meat, one of their first proteins will likely be chicken. Its mild taste can be a benefit. But when baby is ready for more flavor, simply add in an apple and complete the meal with some hearty rice. It all cooks together in the multi-cooker—no cooking in stages.

1 cup long-grain rice

1 boneless, skinless chicken breast

1 cup peeled, cored, and diced apple

1¾ cups chicken broth

1. Place the rice into the multi-cooker; add the chicken and apples on top.

2. Cover the ingredients with the broth; secure the lid.

3. Cook on High Pressure for 10 minutes.

4. When the cook time is complete, turn off the multi-cooker. Let the steam release naturally for 10 minutes, then use the quick release valve to finish releasing the pressure.

5. After the float valve drops, remove the lid carefully.

6. When cool enough to handle, remove the chicken and shred with two forks.

7. Return the chicken to the multi-cooker and mash the mixture to the desired consistency with a fork.

8. Check the temperature before serving.

{ SKIP THE PEELING }

If you want to add even more fiber to this nutrient-packed meal, you can leave the skin on the apple. Just make sure it's mashed well into the mixture, with no large pieces remaining.

BABY RATATOUILLE

Makes 36 ounces • Prep time: 10 minutes • Pressure time: 6 minutes

Don't be frightened by the word *ratatouille*! This baby-friendly dish takes only 6 minutes of pressure time to cook up vegetables similar to the ingredients in the traditional table-food version. It's a sophisticated flavor medley that your multi-cooker makes simple to introduce to your baby.

1 medium zucchini, cut into 1-inch chunks

1 red bell pepper, cored, seeded, and cut into 1-inch chunks

1 medium eggplant, cut into 1-inch chunks

¼ cup water

1 (28-ounce) can diced tomatoes, drained

1 tablespoon olive oil

1. Place the zucchini, bell pepper, eggplant, and water into the multi-cooker; secure the lid.

2. Cook on High Pressure for 6 minutes.

3. When the cook time is complete, turn off the multi-cooker. Use the quick release valve to release the pressure.

4. After the float valve drops, remove the lid carefully.

5. Stir in the tomatoes and olive oil.

6. When cool enough to handle, mash the mixture to the desired consistency with a fork.

7. Check the temperature before serving.

{ ## HEALTHY FAT FACT }

Olive oil is high in healthy fatty acids that your baby's brain uses for development. Just a bit is all that's needed.

CHICKEN + VEGGIE MEDLEY

Makes 48 ounces • Prep time: 5 minutes • Pressure time: 10 minutes

This chicken and veggie combination is a delicious, hearty meal that can work for the whole family! Once the multi-cooker cooks up the magic, puree a portion for your baby. Then mix the rest with cream of chicken soup to fill a pie crust and make chicken pot pie.

2 boneless, skinless chicken breasts	12 ounces frozen vegetable medley	1 cup water

1. Place the chicken, vegetables, and water into the multi-cooker; secure the lid.

2. Cook on High Pressure for 10 minutes.

3. When the cook time is complete, turn off the multi-cooker. Use the quick release valve to release the pressure.

4. After the float valve drops, remove the lid carefully.

5. Remove the chicken and vegetables. Save the water.

6. When cool enough to handle, transfer the mixture to a blender jar or a food processor; puree, adding the reserved water as needed for the desired consistency.

7. Check the temperature before serving.

{ ## FRESH AND READY TO GO }

Vegetables are frozen at the peak of freshness and retain most of their nutrients in the process. So don't feel bad about turning to frozen options. They may be fresher than what you can get at the market for certain choices at certain times of the year.

BEEF STEW

Makes 20 ounces • Prep time: 10 minutes • Pressure time: 18 minutes

Beef stew is a comforting family favorite that you can share with your baby with just a few steps. It boasts a good amount of iron for your little one, too. Keep it chunky or blend to the desired consistency for each baby stage.

---

1 pound beef stew meat, diced

4 carrots, peeled and cut into 1-inch chunks

2 small russet potatoes, peeled and cut into 1-inch cubes

2 tablespoons tomato paste

1 cup water

---

1. Place the beef, carrots, potatoes, tomato paste, and water into the multi-cooker; secure the lid.

2. Cook on High Pressure for 18 minutes.

3. When the cook time is complete, turn off the multi-cooker. Let the steam release naturally for 5 minutes, then use the quick release valve to finish releasing the pressure.

4. After the float valve drops, remove the lid carefully.

5. When cool enough to handle, use a slotted spoon to transfer the mixture to a blender jar or a food processor; save the water. Pulse, adding the reserved water as needed for the desired consistency.

6. Check the temperature before serving.

{ TRY A SPICE }

Oregano would be a perfect spice to add to this stew for additional flavor. Do a taste test with your baby to see which version they like best—plain or gently seasoned.

BEET HUMMUS

Makes 20 ounces • Prep time: 10 minutes • Pressure time: 40 minutes

Who doesn't love a hardworking, nutritious recipe the whole family can enjoy? Your baby will love this hummus as a meal puree. Then transform it into a delicious dip for an older toddler (or anyone!) to enjoy with carrot sticks or other sliced veggies.

---

1 cup dried chickpeas, rinsed

3 cups water

3 tablespoons fresh lemon juice

2 tablespoons olive oil

1 teaspoon ground cumin

4 ounces beet puree (page 47)

---

1. Place the chickpeas and water into the multi-cooker; secure the lid.

2. Cook on High Pressure for 40 minutes.

3. When the cook time is complete, turn off the multi-cooker. Let the steam release naturally for 15 minutes, then use the quick release valve to finish releasing the pressure.

4. After the float valve drops, remove the lid carefully.

5. Drain the chickpeas in a colander, reserving the water, and let cool for 20 minutes.

6. Transfer the chickpeas to a blender jar or a food processor.

7. Add 1 cup of the reserved water to the chickpeas and blend, adding more water as needed for the desired consistency.

8. Add the lemon juice, olive oil, and cumin; blend until smooth.

9. Add the beet puree; pulse to incorporate. Serve.

{ ## COMPLEMENTARY INGREDIENTS }

Chickpeas have a lot of iron, which is great for your baby. When you combine them with lemon juice in this recipe, you increase the benefit. Lemon juice contains vitamin C, which helps iron absorption.

SPAGHETTI + MEAT SAUCE

Makes 24 ounces • Prep time: 1 minute • Pressure time: 6 minutes

In the mood for spaghetti but don't want to be tied to monitoring a pot of water? This recipe is your winner! Ready your favorite sauce without distraction while your multi-cooker makes the pasta. You can also use your favorite store-bought meat sauce if you choose.

8 ounces spaghetti

2 tablespoons unsalted butter

2 cups water

1 cup meat sauce, homemade or store-bought, warmed

1. Place the spaghetti, butter, and water into the multi-cooker, stirring to make sure the pasta is covered with water; secure the lid.
2. Cook on High Pressure for 6 minutes.
3. When the cook time is complete, turn off the multi-cooker. Use the quick release valve to release the pressure.
4. After the float valve drops, remove the lid carefully.
5. Drain the spaghetti in a colander and let cool for 10 minutes.
6. Transfer the spaghetti to a large bowl; top with the sauce.
7. Mash the mixture with a fork, or use an immersion blender to puree to the desired consistency.
8. Check the temperature before serving.

{
MAKE IT MEATLESS
Simply choose a meatless sauce to make this recipe vegetarian.
You can swap in a gluten-free spaghetti option too.
It's always a great idea to adapt recipes for your family's needs!
}

CHOOSE-YOUR-OWN-MEAT PUREE

A simple meat puree can be a delicious way to include iron and protein in your baby's meals. You can batch-cook meat to puree and freeze for baby food, or you can cook meat for your own family meal and just blend a portion to the right puree consistency! Adding in other purees makes for a quick and easy mealtime. Some of our favorite meat puree mix-ins include potato, pea, broccoli, apple, pear, cauliflower, squash, and spinach.

Different meats need different cook times in your multi-cooker. Here is a quick go-to chart for some favorites.

MEAT	COOK TIME ON HIGH PRESSURE
Beef (stew chunks)	20 minutes per 1 pound
Chicken (boneless, skinless breasts)	6–8 minutes per 1 pound
Fish (fillets)	2–3 minutes per 1 pound
Turkey (boneless, skinless breasts)	7–9 minutes per 1 pound

1. Place the meat and 1 cup of water into the multi-cooker; secure the lid.

2. Cook on High Pressure for the appropriate time (see chart).

3. When the cook time is complete, turn off the multi-cooker. Let the steam release naturally for 10 minutes, then use the quick release valve to finish releasing the pressure.

4. After the float valve drops, remove the lid carefully.

5. Once cool enough to handle, transfer the meat to a food processor; save the water. Puree, adding the reserved water as needed for the desired consistency.

CARROT + POTATO + PEA PUREE

Makes 24 ounces • Prep time: 5 minutes • Pressure time: 4 minutes

Carrots and potatoes and peas, oh my! Your little one will enjoy a classic vegetable combination in mashed form. You'll enjoy how quickly this stage 3 meal comes together. It's also very versatile—feel free to switch up the vegetable variety depending on what's in your fridge.

---

1 cup water

4 carrots, peeled and cut into 2-inch pieces

2 medium potatoes, peeled and cut into ¼-inch-thick slices

½ cup frozen peas

---

1. Place the trivet into the multi-cooker; add the water.
2. Add the carrots, potatoes, and peas to a steamer basket.
3. Place the steamer basket on the trivet; secure the lid.
4. Cook on High Pressure for 4 minutes.
5. When the cook time is complete, turn off the multi-cooker. Let the steam release naturally for 5 minutes, then use the quick release valve to finish releasing the pressure.
6. After the float valve drops, remove the lid carefully.
7. Remove the steamer basket and let cool for 10 minutes.
8. Transfer the vegetables to a large bowl; mash to the desired consistency with a fork.
9. Check the temperature before serving.

PERFECT POTATOES

When your little one advances to potatoes in full baked form, your trivet will come in handy. Trivet steaming both regular and sweet potatoes in your multi-cooker gives you amazing results.

HERBED WHITE BEAN PUREE

Makes 40 ounces • Prep time: 5 minutes • Pressure time: 28 minutes

Even though it doesn't contain tahini, this recipe will remind you of a hummus. Use it as a puree now and as a dip when your baby is ready for finger foods. It might be even better than hummus for some households—blending it without tahini makes it perfect for those with a sesame allergy.

2 cups dried white beans, rinsed

2 garlic cloves, peeled

1 teaspoon chopped fresh rosemary

1 teaspoon chopped fresh thyme

8 cups water

¼ cup extra-virgin olive oil

Juice of 1 lemon

1. Place the beans, garlic, rosemary, thyme, and water into the multi-cooker, making sure beans are submerged; secure the lid.

2. Cook on High Pressure for 28 minutes.

3. When the cook time is complete, turn off the multi-cooker. Let the steam release naturally for 20 minutes, then use the quick release valve to finish releasing the pressure.

4. After the float valve drops, remove the lid carefully.

5. Reserve ½ cup of the water. Drain the beans in a colander and let cool for 20 minutes.

6. Transfer the beans to a blender jar or a food processor.

7. Add the olive oil and lemon juice; puree, adding the reserved water as needed for the desired consistency.

8. Transfer to a storage jar or container.

{ RECIPES THAT GROW WITH YOU }

The best baby food recipes can grow with your baby's stages with just simple adjustments. When your child is ready, serve this as a dip with some crackers or fresh cut veggies.

CHUNKY POTATO MASH

Makes 16 ounces • Prep time: 5 minutes • Pressure time: 5 minutes

Nothing warms a body and heart like mashed potatoes. In a multi-cooker you can whip up a batch rather quickly. Just mash with a fork or use a quick pulse of the immersion blender and serve to your toddler who is ready for a next-level food.

1 cup water	2 medium potatoes, peeled and quartered

1. Place a steamer basket into the multi-cooker; add the water.

2. Place the potatoes in the steamer basket; secure the lid.

3. Cook on High Pressure for 5 minutes.

4. When the cook time is complete, turn off the multi-cooker. Use the quick release valve to release the pressure.

5. After the float valve drops, remove the lid carefully.

6. Test with a fork to make sure the potatoes are soft. (If they are still too tough, return to the multi-cooker; secure the lid. Cook on High Pressure for 2 more minutes.)

7. Remove the steamer basket. Let the potatoes cool for 20 minutes.

8. Transfer the potatoes to a medium bowl; mash with a fork to the desired consistency.

9. Check the temperature before serving.

{ ## MASH IT YOUR WAY }

You can use white russet potatoes for a classic mash or sweeten the pot with a sweet potato mash. Want to add a veggie to your mash? Just wash it and place it in the steamer basket in step 2, along with the potatoes.

CORN CHOWDER

Makes 32 ounces • Prep time: 10 minutes • Pressure time: 15 minutes

Bring those sweet flavors of summer to your baby's bowl and your dinner table in record time with this corn chowder recipe. The grown-ups in your family will think it's the perfect pick-me-up on a dreary day, but kids love it any day of the year!

2 medium red potatoes, peeled and cut into ½-inch chunks 1½ cups whole kernel corn	2 small garlic cloves, minced 1 (14½-ounce) can chicken broth ½ cup half-and-half	1 tablespoon cornstarch ½ cup shredded cheddar cheese Small handful fresh parsley, chopped

1. Place the potatoes, corn, garlic, and broth into the multi-cooker; secure the lid.

2. Cook on High Pressure for 15 minutes.

3. When the cook time is complete, turn off the multi-cooker. Use the quick release valve to release the pressure.

4. After the float valve drops, remove the lid carefully.

5. Press Sauté; adjust to low heat.

6. Add the half-and-half and cornstarch; stir until smooth.

7. Cook, stirring often, until slightly thickened, 6 to 8 minutes.

8. Add the cheese; stir until melted. Puree with an immersion blender to the desired consistency.

9. Sprinkle with the parsley.

10. Check the temperature before serving.

THE PERKS OF PARSLEY

Parsley is one of the most popular herbs in the world and is often used a remedy for digestive issues. It's also rich in antioxidants. So go ahead and toss it in your baby's purees!

SPICED PEAR + DATES + OATS PUREE

Makes 24 ounces • Prep time: 5 minutes • Pressure time: 4 minutes

One way to sweeten up the morning routine is by adding some dates to the mix. But it's not just taste they bring to the table. Dates contain antioxidants and choline, a brain-boosting nutrient important for young children. Because not all oatmeal is gluten free (due to cross contamination), check oat labels if needed.

---

1 cup old fashioned oats

2½ cups water

3 small pears, peeled, cored, and quartered

½ cup pitted dates

1 teaspoon ground nutmeg or cinnamon (optional)

---

1. Pour the oats into the multi-cooker, then add the water.

2. Insert the trivet.

3. Add the pears, dates, and spice (if using) to a steamer basket and place on top of the trivet; secure the lid.

4. Cook on High Pressure for 4 minutes.

5. When the cook time is complete, turn off the multi-cooker. Let the steam release naturally for 10 minutes, then use the quick release valve to finish releasing the pressure.

6. After the float valve drops, remove the lid carefully.

7. Remove the steamer basket and let the mixture cool for 5 minutes.

8. Add the fruit to the multi-cooker and, using an immersion blender, puree the mixture.

9. Transfer the puree to a storage jar or container.

SWEET TREATS

Another way for your baby to enjoy dates right now: in a puree mixed with plain yogurt. Because dates can be sticky, clean your little one's teeth after enjoying. A drink can also help wash away natural sugars.

CHICKEN PASTA

Makes 24 ounces • Prep time: 10 minutes • Pressure time: 6 minutes

Making chicken in the multi-cooker delivers tender, juicy, and full-of-flavor meat that will be easy to pull apart for your little one to eat. Add pasta and you've got a hearty, filling dish. You can leave these as finger foods or blend to your desired consistency.

4 ounces boneless, skinless chicken breast, cut into very small pieces

7 ounces macaroni pasta

3 cups chicken broth

1. Place the chicken into the multi-cooker.
2. Add the pasta and broth, making sure the pasta is completely submerged; secure the lid.
3. Cook on High Pressure for 6 minutes.
4. When the cook time is complete, turn off the multi-cooker. Use the quick release valve to release the pressure.
5. After the float valve drops, remove the lid carefully.
6. Let the mixture cool for 10 minutes.
7. Mash with a fork or puree with an immersion blender to the desired consistency.
8. Check the temperature before serving.

{ ## VEGGIE VARIETY

Pull a pureed vegetable cube out of the freezer to thaw and mix in after the chicken and pasta are cooked. Butternut squash, cauliflower, and broccoli are all great additions, but you can use any flavor. }

BROCCOLI + PEA PENNE

Makes 16 ounces • Prep time: 5 minutes • Pressure time: 6 minutes

Pasta is often a favorite for younger children—and the "big kids" too. To make it more nutritious, it's easy to add a vitamin boost with superfoods such as broccoli and peas. A bit of fat from the butter makes the dish tasty and the vitamins easier to absorb.

---

8 ounces penne pasta

1 cup frozen peas

1 cup broccoli florets

2 tablespoons unsalted butter

2 cups water

---

1. Place the pasta, peas, broccoli, butter, and water into the multi-cooker, making sure the pasta is completely submerged; secure the lid.

2. Cook on High Pressure for 6 minutes.

3. When the cook time is complete, turn off the multi-cooker. Use the quick release valve to release the pressure.

4. After the float valve drops, remove the lid carefully.

5. Let the mixture cool for 10 minutes.

6. Mash with a fork or puree with an immersion blender to the desired consistency.

7. Check the temperature before serving.

{
PICK YOUR PASTA

You can substitute any shape of pasta in this dish;
just choose your family's favorite.
}

YAM + YOGURT + BANANA BLEND

Makes 32–40 ounces • Prep time: 5 minutes • Pressure time: 15 minutes

It's not pie, it's not pie, it's not pie. You may need to repeat this to yourself as you feed your little one. It sure is close, especially if you add a pinch of cinnamon and nutmeg. Or even better, add a dash of anti-inflammatory support with cloves, for an exploring baby's quintessential bumps and bruises.

| 1 cup water | 2 large yams, peeled and cut into ¼-inch-thick slices | 1 cup plain yogurt |
| | | 1 banana |

1. Place the trivet into the multi-cooker; add the water.

2. Place the yam slices on the trivet; secure the lid.

3. Cook on High Pressure for 15 minutes.

4. When the cook time is complete, turn off the multi-cooker. Let the steam release naturally for 10 minutes, then use the quick release valve to finish releasing the pressure.

5. After the float valve drops, remove the lid carefully.

6. With a slotted spoon, remove the yam slices to a medium bowl and let cool for 20 minutes. Save the water.

7. Place the yam slices into a blender jar or a food processor.

8. Add ½ to ¾ cup of the reserved water to the yams. Blend the mixture, adding more water as needed for the desired consistency.

9. Add the yogurt; blend to the desired consistency.

10. Mash the banana with a fork; stir in to yam mixture.

11. Transfer to a storage jar or container.

BROCCOLI-CAULIFLOWER MAC + CHEESE

Makes 32 ounces • Prep time: 5 minutes • Pressure time: 6 minutes

Making luscious macaroni and cheese is super-easy with the help of your multi-cooker! Steamed vegetables add texture and sneak in nutrition with very little extra work. Not serving right away? This dish will hold with the Warm function.

8 ounces macaroni pasta

2 tablespoons unsalted butter

2 cups water

1 cup broccoli florets

1 cup cauliflower florets

¾ cup whole milk

2 ounces shredded mozzarella cheese

4 ounces shredded cheddar cheese

1. Place the pasta, butter, and water into the multi-cooker, making sure the pasta is completely submerged.
2. Add the broccoli and cauliflower; secure the lid.
3. Cook on High Pressure for 6 minutes.
4. When the cook time is complete, turn off the multi-cooker. Use the quick release valve to release the pressure.
5. After the float valve drops, remove the lid carefully.
6. Add the milk; stir well.
7. Add the mozzarella and cheddar cheeses; stir until completely melted.
8. Mash with a fork or puree with an immersion blender to the desired consistency.
9. Check the temperature before serving.

{ ## ANOTHER VEGGIE VERSION

Instead of broccoli and cauliflower, add a cube of thawed Butternut Squash Puree (page 42) when you add in the cheeses. }

TURKEY + PUMPKIN PUREE

Makes 48 ounces • Prep time: 10 minutes • Pressure time: 15 minutes

How wonderful is it when the family gathers around the table for Thanksgiving dinner! Every time you make a batch of this puree for your baby, you're likely to feel the holiday vibe. You can also feel good knowing that pumpkin is loaded with nutrients.

---

2 pounds boneless, skinless turkey breast

1½ cups water

1 (3- to 4-pound) sugar pumpkin or pie pumpkin, peeled, seeded, and cut into 1-inch cubes

---

1. Place the turkey into the multi-cooker; add the water.

2. Insert the trivet into the multi-cooker.

3. Place the pumpkin cubes on the trivet; secure the lid.

4. Cook on High Pressure for 15 minutes.

5. When the cook time is complete, turn off the multi-cooker. Let the steam release naturally for 5 minutes, then use the quick release valve to finish releasing the pressure.

6. After the float valve drops, remove the lid carefully.

7. Test the pumpkin's tenderness with a fork. Cook longer in increments of 5 minutes, repeating the tenderness test and additional steaming as needed.

8. When tender and cool enough to handle, transfer the turkey and pumpkin to a blender jar or a food processor; save the water.

9. Puree, adding the reserved water as needed for the desired consistency.

10. Check the temperature before serving.

{ ## READY FOR A FEAST }

If your family enjoys pumpkin, keep one on hand. Kept in a cool area with plenty of circulating air, a whole, fresh pumpkin lasts two to three months.

BLUEBERRY + PEAR + CHICKPEA PUREE WITH ROSEMARY

Makes 32 ounces • Prep time: 10 minutes • Pressure time: 44 minutes

Chickpeas are a good way to add meatless protein to a little one's diet. Pears offer that deliciously mild sweetness and are full of fiber. Throw in a handful of blueberries and you have a trifecta of flavor and lots of good fuel for a growing immune system.

1 cup dried chickpeas, rinsed

3¾ cups water, divided

2 large pears, peeled, cored, and quartered

½ cup fresh blueberries

Pinch of finely chopped fresh rosemary

1. Place the chickpeas and 3 cups of the water into the multi-cooker; secure the lid.

2. Cook on High Pressure for 40 minutes.

3. When the cook time is complete, turn off the multi-cooker. Let the steam release naturally for 15 minutes, then use the quick release valve to finish releasing the pressure.

4. After the float valve drops, remove the lid carefully.

5. Drain the chickpeas in a colander and let cool for 20 minutes. Discard the water.

6. Place the pears, blueberries, rosemary, and remaining ¾ cup water into the multi-cooker; secure the lid.

7. Cook on High Pressure for 4 minutes.

8. When the cook time is complete, turn off the multi-cooker. Let the steam release naturally for 5 minutes, then use the quick release valve to finish releasing the pressure.

9. After the float valve drops, remove the lid carefully.

10. Remove the mixture to a small bowl and let cool for 5 minutes. Save the water.

11. Transfer the chickpeas, pears, blueberries, and rosemary to a blender jar; puree, adding the reserved water as needed for the desired consistency.

LEMON RISOTTO

Makes 44 ounces • Prep time: 5 minutes • Pressure time: 6 minutes

This dish is bursting with flavor from the addition of lemon. The texture makes for a great finger food or practice for your little one's spoon skills. The rice is thick and slightly sticky, so they'll at least get some into their mouth. Add water, formula, or breast milk to thin if needed when blending for a puree.

2 tablespoons olive oil

1½ cups Arborio rice

4 cups chicken broth

½ cup grated Parmesan cheese

1 tablespoon unsalted butter

Zest of 1 lemon

1–2 tablespoons lemon juice

Freshly ground black pepper, to taste

1. Add the olive oil to the multi-cooker; press Sauté.

2. Add the rice; sauté for 3 minutes.

3. Turn off the multi-cooker.

4. Add the broth; secure the lid.

5. Cook on High Pressure for 6 minutes.

6. When the cook time is complete, turn off the multi-cooker. Use the quick release valve to release the pressure.

7. After the float valve drops, remove the lid carefully.

8. Add the cheese and butter, stirring for 2 to 3 minutes until the mixture thickens.

9. Add the lemon zest, lemon juice, and black pepper.

10. Using an immersion blender, puree in the multi-cooker to the desired consistency.

11. Check the temperature before serving.

{ ## EASY ADJUSTMENT }

Feel free to substitute quinoa, farro, or brown rice for the Arborio rice. There are so many great grains for your baby to try!

CARROT-COCONUT QUINOA

Makes 8 ounces • Prep time: 5 minutes • Pressure time: 4 minutes

The great thing about quinoa is that it's an easy 1:1 ratio of grain to liquid when cooking in your multi-cooker. My family likes to add coconut milk to infuse it with a creamy, tropical flavor. The recipe calls for tossing in a few fresh carrots, but you can also use premade carrot puree if you have some in the freezer.

1 cup dried quinoa, rinsed	1 cup coconut milk	2 carrots, peeled and cut into 2-inch pieces

1. Place the quinoa and coconut milk into the multi-cooker; add the carrots on top. Secure the lid.

2. Cook on High Pressure for 4 minutes.

3. When the cook time is complete, turn off the multi-cooker. Let the steam release naturally for 10 minutes, then use the quick release valve to finish releasing the pressure.

4. After the float valve drops, remove the lid carefully.

5. When cool enough to handle, puree the mixture right in the multi-cooker with an immersion blender.

6. Check the temperature before serving.

THE COCONUT KICK

Coconut milk not only tastes great, but it also provides a good amount of healthy fat. It can be connected to some tree nut allergies, so be sure to test it alone or along with other cleared foods first.

STAGE 4

FIRST FINGER FOODS

BANANA-BLUEBERRY MUFFIN BITES

Makes 14 muffin bites • Prep time: 10 minutes • Pressure time: 12 minutes

Naturally sweetened with fruit and just a touch of vanilla, these muffin bites make super first finger foods, but they're also yummy and nourishing for kids of any age. Blueberries rock as antioxidant sources; they also deliver a good amount of fiber. Research has connected the little blue gems with many heart-health benefits.

2 medium bananas

2 large eggs

¼ cup vegetable oil or melted coconut oil

1 teaspoon vanilla extract

¾ cup all-purpose flour

1½ teaspoons baking powder

1 cup blueberries

½ cup water

1. In a large mixing bowl, mash the bananas with a fork.

2. Add the eggs, oil, and vanilla. Beat with a handheld mixer until the mixture is smooth and slightly frothy.

3. Add the flour and baking powder and beat until well combined.

4. Coat two 7-cup egg bite mold pans with nonstick spray. Divide the batter evenly among the cups. Add blueberries to each cup, pressing them into the batter. Cover the pans with aluminum foil; set aside.

5. Place the trivet into the multi-cooker; add the water.

6. Stack the pans on the trivet; secure the lid.

7. Cook on High Pressure for 12 minutes.

8. When the cook time is complete, turn off the multi-cooker. Let the steam release naturally for 5 minutes, then use the quick release valve to finish releasing the pressure.

9. After the float valve drops, remove the lid carefully. Lift out the pans with oven mitts.

10. Transfer the muffin bites to a plate. Let cool for 5 minutes before serving.

CRANBERRY MUFFIN BITES

Makes 20 bites • Prep time: 10 minutes • Pressure time: 10 minutes per batch

Easy first finger foods, these sweet little packages introduce cranberries—full of antioxidants and rich in several vitamins and minerals, especially vitamin C. To make the bites, work in batches. Most egg bite molds have seven cups and you can use up to two molds per batch in your multi-cooker if you use the egg molds that stack.

2 cups all-purpose flour	½ teaspoon salt	¾ cup orange juice
1 teaspoon baking powder	2 eggs	1 cup frozen cranberries, thawed
½ teaspoon baking soda	5 tablespoons unsalted butter, melted	1 cup water

1. In a large bowl, combine the flour, baking powder, baking soda, and salt.

2. In a separate large bowl, whisk together the eggs, butter, and orange juice.

3. Add the dry ingredients to the wet ingredients in batches, thoroughly mixing after each addition.

4. Coat two 7-cup egg bite mold pans with nonstick spray. Use a teaspoon to fill each mold halfway with batter. Divide two-thirds of the cranberries evenly among the cups, pressing them into the batter. Cover the pans with aluminum foil; set aside.

5. Place the trivet into the multi-cooker; add the water.

6. Stack the pans on the trivet; secure the lid.

7. Cook on High Pressure for 10 minutes.

8. When the cook time is complete, turn off the multi-cooker. Let the steam release naturally for 5 minutes, then use the quick release valve to finish releasing the pressure.

9. After the float valve drops, remove the lid carefully. Lift out the pans with oven mitts.

10. Transfer the muffin bites to a plate. Repeat with the remaining batter.

11. Let cool for 5 minutes before serving.

EASY FRITTATA

Makes 8 servings • Prep time: 5 minutes • Pressure time: 25 minutes

This simple egg frittata has a smooth texture to help your beginning table-food eater. But once your baby gets going, you can use this recipe as a starting point and add whatever vegetables you like. Cut a slice of frittata into smaller pieces for your little one to enjoy as a complete source of protein—eggs contain all nine essential amino acids.

1½ cups water
6 large eggs

½ cup milk

1. Place the trivet into the multi-cooker; add the water.
2. Spray a 5-inch round ramekin with nonstick spray.
3. In a bowl, whisk the eggs and milk; pour into the ramekin.
4. Using a sling, lower the ramekin onto the trivet; secure the lid.
5. Cook on Soup setting for 25 minutes.

6. When the cook time is complete, turn off the multi-cooker. Let the steam release naturally for 5 minutes, then use the quick release valve to finish releasing the pressure.
7. After the float valve drops, remove the lid carefully. Lift out the pan with oven mitts.
8. With a paper towel, blot any liquid that has formed on the top of the frittata.
9. Let cool for 5 minutes before slicing and serving.

{ ## ADD-IN IDEAS

Need flavor ideas for a frittata? Try thawed frozen spinach, chopped broccoli, chopped asparagus, or diced sun-dried tomatoes. }

BANANA BREAD

Makes 18 servings • Prep time: 10 minutes • Pressure time: 50 minutes

Don't toss those browning bananas—turn them into a simple and yummy finger food! Just the smell of banana bread in the air will get everyone excited for the first taste. And every moist bite is perfect for a new table-food eater.

1½ cups water	2 eggs	1 teaspoon vanilla extract
2 cups all-purpose flour	¼ cup vegetable oil or melted coconut oil	3 very ripe bananas, mashed
¾ teaspoon baking powder		

1. Place the trivet into the multi-cooker; add the water.

2. Spray a 7-inch round cake pan with nonstick spray.

3. In a large bowl, combine the flour and baking powder.

4. In a separate large bowl, whisk the eggs, oil, and vanilla.

5. Add the dry ingredients to the wet ingredients in batches, thoroughly mixing after each addition.

6. Stir in the bananas.

7. Pour the batter into the cake pan. Using a sling, lower the pan onto the trivet; secure the lid.

8. Cook on High Pressure for 50 minutes.

9. When the cook time is complete, turn off the multi-cooker. Let the steam release naturally for 5 minutes, then use the quick release valve to finish releasing the pressure.

10. After the float valve drops, remove the lid carefully. Lift out the pan with oven mitts.

11. With a paper towel, blot any liquid that has formed on the top of the bread.

12. Let cool for 5 minutes before slicing and serving.

HARD-BOILED EGGS

Makes 7 eggs • Prep time: 1 minute • Pressure time: 10 minutes

Making hard-boiled eggs is simple in the multi-cooker. Cut into pieces, they make great finger food that kids love! And the nutrition is smart as well. The humble egg is often called the perfect food because of its protein, vitamins, and minerals.

1 cup water	7 eggs

1. Place an egg trivet into the multi-cooker; add the water.

2. Place an egg into each section of the trivet; secure the lid.

3. Cook on High Pressure for 10 minutes.

4. When the cook time is complete, turn off the multi-cooker. Let the steam release naturally for 10 minutes, then use the quick release valve to finish releasing the pressure.

5. After the float valve drops, remove the lid carefully.

6. Transfer the eggs to an ice-water bath and let them cool for 5 minutes.

7. Peel the eggs before serving.

{ ## PEELING TRICK

Place a hard-boiled egg in a small glass. Place your hand over the top of the glass and shake rapidly with two hands for 5 seconds. The eggshell should come off quite easily. }

APPLE BUTTER

Makes 32 ounces • Prep time: 10 minutes • Pressure time: 20 minutes

Apple butter is a great addition to your baby food pantry. This no-sugar-added spread is great for toast and sandwiches, in yogurt or oatmeal, or even just eating with a spoon! It can also be used in recipes for a sweet, healthier alternative to store-bought jellies.

---

8 apples, peeled, cored, and quartered

½ cup water

½ teaspoon ground cinnamon

⅛ teaspoon ground cloves

⅛ teaspoon ground nutmeg

⅛ teaspoon vanilla extract

---

1. Place the apples and water into the multi-cooker; secure the lid.

2. Cook on High Pressure for 20 minutes.

3. When the cook time is complete, turn off the multi-cooker. Let the steam release naturally for 10 minutes, then use the quick release valve to finish releasing the pressure.

4. After the float valve drops, remove the lid carefully.

5. Add the cinnamon, cloves, nutmeg, and vanilla.

6. Using an immersion blender, puree the mixture. To thicken, simmer on the Sauté setting to the desired consistency.

7. Transfer the butter to a storage jar or container.

{ ## STORE IT RIGHT

Although it may get eaten up very quickly, you can refrigerate your apple butter for up to 1 week or freeze for up to 1 year. }

PUMPKIN + WHITE BEAN SOUP

Makes 48 ounces • Prep time: 5 minutes • Pressure time: 25 minutes

Give your baby's immune system a boost with this stage 4 soup! Pumpkin is full of nutrients, especially vitamin A and fiber. This recipe makes enough for the entire family to enjoy together.

2 (15-ounce) cans great Northern beans, drained and rinsed

1 (15-ounce) can pumpkin puree

2 cups vegetable broth

1 teaspoon dried oregano

1. Place the beans, pumpkin, broth, and oregano into the multi-cooker; secure the lid.

2. Cook on the Soup setting for 25 minutes.

3. When the cook time is complete, turn off the multi-cooker. Let the steam release naturally for 12 minutes, then use the quick release valve to finish releasing the pressure.

4. After the float valve drops, remove the lid carefully.

5. Check the temperature before serving.

{ CHOOSE WHAT WORKS

For the pumpkin puree, you can use one 15-ounce can or 15 ounces of your own homemade Pumpkin Puree (page 32). For a fancier touch, garnish the soup with sliced or diced fresh avocado. }

SUMMER VEGETABLE PASTA

Makes 24 ounces • Prep time: 10 minutes • Pressure time: 6 minutes

Green veggies are superfoods that taste fabulous combined with pasta. Zucchini and asparagus lend a fresh taste of summer's goodness while also giving you flexibility for the food stage your baby is in. Keep them bite-size for great finger foods or easily blend them for a chunky puree.

8 ounces small pasta, such as orzo, farfalle, ditalini, or orecchiette

2 cups water

6 asparagus spears, trimmed and cut into 1-inch pieces

½ small zucchini, peeled and cut into ½-inch chunks

2 basil leaves

1. Place the pasta, water, asparagus, zucchini, and basil into the multi-cooker, stirring to make sure the pasta is submerged; secure the lid.

2. Cook on High Pressure for 6 minutes.

3. When the cook time is complete, turn off the multi-cooker. Use the quick release valve to release the pressure.

4. After the float valve drops, remove the lid carefully.

5. Drain the mixture in a colander and let cool for 10 minutes. Discard the basil leaves.

6. Check the temperature before serving.

{ Say Cheese? }

My family loves a sprinkle of Parmesan cheese on top on this pasta recipe, but it's also delicious without for families not consuming dairy.

YAM FRIES

Makes 8 servings • Prep time: 20 minutes • Pressure time: 30 minutes

Who says "baby food" needs to be boring? As your baby's eating abilities and tastes develop, it's fun to try a little more flavor. Here's a side dish everyone in the family will eat up! Adjust the seasonings based on your family's preferences—there's no right or wrong way.

4 tablespoons olive oil

1 tablespoon dried ground rosemary

2 teaspoons smoked paprika

¼–½ teaspoon cayenne pepper

6 yams, peeled and cut into long, 1/4-inch-thick fries

1 cup water

1. In a large bowl, combine the olive oil, rosemary, smoked paprika, and cayenne; add the yams, toss to coat, and let marinate for 20 minutes.

2. Place the trivet into the multi-cooker; add the water.

3. Place the yams on the trivet; secure the lid.

4. Cook on High Pressure for 30 minutes.

5. When the cook time is complete, turn off the multi-cooker. Let the steam release naturally for 10 minutes, then use the quick release valve to finish releasing the pressure.

6. After the float valve drops, remove the lid carefully.

7. Check the temperature before serving.

{ YAMS VS. SWEET POTATOES }

Yams and sweet potatoes are sometimes confused, but there is a difference! If you're having trouble finding yams in your local market, try an international market or ethnic food stores.

CHICKEN FRIED RICE

Makes 28 ounces • Prep time: 5 minutes • Pressure time: 10 minutes

Rice dinners make great dishes for little fingers to pick up. But your baby won't be the only one in the family thrilled with chicken fried rice, a takeout favorite that's even better when you can prep it quickly and healthfully at home.

---

1 yellow onion, finely chopped (optional)

1 cup dry long-grain rice

1 boneless, skinless chicken breast

1¾ cups chicken broth

1 tablespoon olive oil

1 cup frozen pea/carrot medley

---

1. Place the onion (if using) and the rice into the multi-cooker, then add the chicken and broth on top. Secure the lid.

2. Cook on High Pressure for 10 minutes.

3. When the cook time is complete, turn off the multi-cooker. Let the steam release naturally for 10 minutes, then use the quick release valve to finish releasing the pressure.

4. After the float valve drops, remove the lid carefully.

5. When cool enough to handle, remove the chicken and shred with two forks; set aside.

6. Move the rice to one side of the multi-cooker; set to Sauté.

7. Add the oil to the empty side of the multi-cooker, then add the peas and carrots. Cook for 2 minutes, stirring.

8. Turn off the multi-cooker. Return the chicken to the multi-cooker and stir to combine.

9. Check the temperature before serving.

{ PLAY DATE PLANNED? }

Another benefit to this recipe: it's easy to double to feed a crowd. Just check for any allergies or food preferences before guests arrive.

CHEESY SPINACH PASTA

Makes 16 ounces • Prep time: 5 minutes • Pressure time: 6 minutes

Everyone loves a cheesy pasta! Although a simple recipe, it becomes a fancy affair with bow tie noodle fun. You can swap in any type of small pasta, and go ahead and add more or different types of cheese to suit your family's tastes. Whatever you choose, it will be the perfect pasta for you.

8 ounces bow tie pasta

2 tablespoons unsalted butter

2 cups water

¾ cup whole milk

4 ounces shredded cheddar cheese

2 ounces shredded mozzarella cheese

1 cup fresh spinach

1. Place the pasta, butter, and water into the multi-cooker, stirring to make sure the pasta is submerged; secure the lid.

2. Cook on High Pressure for 6 minutes.

3. When the cook time is complete, turn off the multi-cooker. Use the quick release valve to release the pressure.

4. After the float valve drops, remove the lid carefully. Drain the mixture in a colander if any water remains.

5. Stir in the milk, then add the cheddar and mozzarella, stirring until completely melted.

6. Add the spinach and stir until wilted.

7. Check the temperature before serving.

GREAT DINNER FOR A BUSY DAY

This recipe holds on the Warm setting of your multi-cooker very well. So if it's one of those days when you need to prep it early or the family needs to eat in shifts, it will be a dinner dream come true.

TURKEY MEATBALLS + RICE

Makes 7 meatballs + 8 ounces rice • Prep time: 10 minutes •
Pressure time: 10 minutes

Meatballs are a simply delicious, protein-powered meal for families at all stages. Start with just the basics, and then as your little one grows, add in flavorful flair with garlic, onion, grated Parmesan, and lemon zest. Because not all oatmeal is gluten free (due to cross contamination), check oat labels if needed.

½ cup dry white rice

1 cup water

8 ounces lean ground turkey

½ cup old fashioned oats, pulsed to rice-size pieces in a blender

1 egg, lightly beaten

1 teaspoon dried oregano

1. Place the rice and water into the multi-cooker; insert the egg trivet.

2. Spray an egg bite mold pan with nonstick spray; place the mold on the trivet.

3. In a large bowl, combine the turkey, oats, egg, and oregano.

4. Divide the turkey mixture into seven equal portions; roll each portion into a ball. Place one meatball in each section of the egg mold; the balls may be higher than the mold.

5. Secure the lid. Cook on High Pressure for 10 minutes.

6. When the cook time is complete, turn off the multi-cooker. Let the steam release naturally for 10 minutes, then use the quick release valve to finish releasing the pressure.

7. After the float valve drops, remove the lid carefully.

8. Remove the meatballs. Stir the rice before serving.

{ ## BEYOND TURKEY }

My family loves ground turkey. But feel free to sub in your meat of choice, or what you have on hand. Ground beef, ground chicken, and ground pork all work well.

SALMON + RICE

Salmon and rice is a good finger food combination for a growing mind and body. Salmon offers a good source of protein and essential fatty acids (great for brain development) as well as vitamins A and D and multiple B vitamins. Rice is very easy to digest and a source of protein, too! Add in peas for a complete meal.

½ **cup dry white rice**

1 cup water

1 (8-ounce) salmon fillet (fresh or thawed)

1. Place the rice and water into the multi-cooker; insert the trivet.
2. Place the salmon on the trivet; secure the lid.
3. Cook on High Pressure for 5 minutes.
4. When the cook time is complete, turn off the multi-cooker. Use the quick release valve to release the pressure.
5. After the float valve drops, remove the lid carefully.
6. Remove the salmon and rice immediately; check the temperature before serving.

{ ## SAFE WATERS

Salmon is a low-mercury fish, making it safe for your baby to enjoy up to two or three times per week. }

MEATLOAF + MASHED POTATOES

Makes 6 servings • Prep time: 15 minutes • Pressure time: 25 minutes

This classic pairing is easy to make in the multi-cooker for a family meal. Your baby will enjoy the meat crumbled as finger food and have fun practicing scooping skills with the mashed potatoes. Have the camera ready as you enjoy little smiles full of potatoes!

2½ pounds potatoes, peeled and quartered

1½ cups chicken broth

2 pounds ground beef

½ cup bread crumbs

2 eggs, lightly beaten

⅓ cup milk

⅓ cup ketchup

1½ teaspoons garlic powder

½ teaspoon dried oregano

¼ teaspoon dried thyme

4 tablespoons unsalted butter

½ cup half-and-half

1. Place the potatoes and broth into the multi-cooker; insert the trivet.

2. In a large bowl, combine the ground beef, bread crumbs, eggs, milk, ketchup, garlic power, oregano, and thyme.

3. Coat a 7-inch cake pan with nonstick spray, then add the meatloaf mixture. Using a sling, lower the pan onto the trivet.

4. Secure the lid; cook on High Pressure for 25 minutes.

5. When the cook time is complete, turn off the multi-cooker. Let the steam release naturally for 10 minutes, then use the quick release valve to finish releasing the pressure.

6. After the float valve drops, remove the lid carefully.

7. Using a turkey baster, suction off most of the meatloaf drippings so the hot liquid doesn't spill over when removing the pan.

8. Using the sling, remove the pan from the multi-cooker. Flip the meatloaf out of the pan onto a large plate.

9. Add the butter and half-and-half to the potatoes in the multi-cooker; mash or puree with an immersion blender.

10. Slice the meatloaf and serve with the potatoes.

CHICKEN NOODLE SOUP

Makes 72 ounces • Prep time: 10 minutes • Pressure time: 10 minutes

Nothing quite meets the need for comfort (at any age) like chicken noodle soup. But a pot simmering on the stove doesn't always fit into a family's schedule. You can have all the homemade goodness of soft noodles and tender chicken from your multi-cooker in just minutes!

2 boneless, skinless chicken breasts

1 cup peeled and chopped carrots

1 cup chopped celery

1 tablespoon chopped parsley

1 bay leaf

6 cups chicken broth

4 ounces egg noodles (about 2½ cups)

1. Place the chicken, carrots, celery, parsley, bay leaf, and broth into the multi-cooker; secure the lid.

2. Cook on the Soup setting for 10 minutes.

3. When the cook time is complete, turn off the multi-cooker. Let the steam release naturally for 10 minutes, then use the quick release valve to finish releasing the pressure.

4. After the float valve drops, remove the lid carefully. Discard the bay leaf.

5. When cool enough to handle, remove the chicken and shred with two forks.

6. Set the multi-cooker to Sauté. When the broth begins to boil, add the noodles and allow them to simmer until tender, 6 to 8 minutes.

7. Turn off the multi-cooker. Return the chicken to the pot.

8. Check the temperature before serving.

STAGE BY STAGE

Give your baby only what they can handle right now. Use a slotted spoon to serve just the chicken, noodles, and veggies to younger eaters. As your little one is ready for more, leave a little broth.

HAM + PEA SOUP

Makes 32 ounces • Prep time: 5 minutes • Pressure time: 4 minutes

No waste, great taste! If you're a frugal family like we are, you'll love using leftover ham in this soup. The kids love ham for the first dinner served with sides and again later in the week when it transforms into the soup du jour.

1 cup chopped cooked ham	12 ounces frozen peas ½ cup chicken broth	½ cup water

1. Place the ham, peas, broth, and water into the multi-cooker; secure the lid.

2. Cook on High Pressure for 4 minutes.

3. When the cook time is complete, turn off the multi-cooker. Let the steam release naturally for 5 minutes, then use the quick release valve to finish releasing the pressure.

4. After the float valve drops, remove the lid carefully.

5. Check the temperature before serving.

{ SOUP ON THE MENU }

Any precooked meat can be used to make a simple soup. Any veggie can be substituted as well. Choose a different soup each week if you like.

CARROT STICKS

Makes 16 to 24 ounces • Prep time: 5 minutes • Pressure time: 4 minutes

Is your baby watching the big kids and grown-ups munch carrots and dip? It's easy to include beginning eaters in the dipping party! Just toss some carrots in the multi-cooker for a quick steam and they're ready for easier bites of finger food as your baby masters chewing.

---

1 cup water

8 carrots, peeled and cut into sticks

---

1. Place a steamer basket into the multi-cooker; add the water.

2. Add the carrots; secure the lid.

3. Cook on High Pressure for 4 minutes.

4. When the cook time is complete, turn off the multi-cooker. Let the steam release naturally for 5 minutes, then use the quick release valve to finish releasing the pressure.

5. After the float valve drops, remove the lid carefully.

6. Let the carrots cool for 20 minutes before serving.

{ ## DELICIOUS DIPS }

Carrots are sweet finger foods alone, but for extra feeding fun, serve them with a dip. Try Beet Hummus (page 101) or Herbed White Bean Puree (page 107).

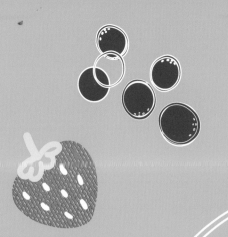

BONUS

SENSATIONAL SMOOTHIES

Sure, this is a baby food cookbook, but you can also use your fruit and vegetable purees to make nutrient-packed smoothies. With our busy household schedule, I love a creamy smoothie to give the whole family a quick and easy start to the day or an infusion of vitamins at lunch. Pour a cup for yourself and share the rest in a sippy cup or kid-friendly cup with a straw for your little one!

AVOCADO-SPINACH SMOOTHIE

Makes 16 ounces • Prep time: 5 minutes

Almost more like a milkshake, this smoothie is a luscious dream. The banana creates a creamy, naturally sweet base. Then avocado adds fiber, healthy fats, thickness, and depth of flavor. Spinach is always a super addition! Feel free to add in tropical flavors with a couple cubes of frozen mango puree and coconut water instead of milk.

1 banana

½ avocado, pitted and scooped

2 (1-ounce) cubes frozen spinach puree (page 29)

1¼ cups milk of your choice

Juice of ½ lime

3 tablespoons plain yogurt, homemade (page 49) or store-bought

Grown-up topping options: coconut flakes, sliced almonds, or cacao nibs

1. Place the banana, avocado, spinach, milk, lime juice, and yogurt in a blender jar or food processor; blend to the desired consistency.

2. Add any desired toppings for grown-ups. Serve.

SWEET POTATO-PEAR SMOOTHIE

Makes 16 ounces • Prep time: 5 minutes

Yes, you can have a holiday pie in a glass! One taste of this smoothie will convince you. Sweet potato provides the thick, silky creaminess and vitamin-rich base while pear balances with its mild sweetness. With the addition of anti-inflammatory ginger and turmeric, the flavor package is complete.

4 (1-ounce) cubes frozen sweet potato puree (page 21)

4 (1-ounce) cubes frozen pear puree (page 38)

1 cup milk of your choice

½ cup plain yogurt, homemade (page 49) or store-bought

2 or 3 pitted dates

¼ teaspoon ground ginger

¼ teaspoon ground turmeric

¼ teaspoon ground cinnamon

Grown-up topping options: pomegranate arils or pumpkin seeds

1. Place the sweet potato, pear, milk, yogurt, dates, ginger, turmeric, and cinnamon in a blender jar or food processor; blend to the desired consistency.

2. Add any desired toppings for grown-ups. Serve.

POSTPARTUM SMOOTHIE

Makes 20 ounces • Prep time: 5 minutes

As a mom of six, I know that first year in baby's life requires a lot from you—from sleep deprivation to the demands of nursing. The body is strong and can handle a lot, but it helps when we fuel it well, too. This smoothie helps with electrolyte and nutrient replacements.

1 cup coconut water

1 serving vanilla protein powder (according to package)

1 serving collagen powder (according to package)

1 teaspoon bee pollen

1 serving MCT oil (according to package)

½ cup rolled oats

6 (1-ounce) cubes frozen mango and/or peach (pages 20 and 24)

4 (1-ounce) cubes frozen spinach (page 29)

1 banana

1. Place the coconut water, protein powder, collagen powder, bee pollen, MCT oil, rolled oats, peach and/or mango, spinach, and banana in a blender jar or food processor; blend to the desired consistency.

2. Give yourself a moment to relax, recharge, and enjoy!

INDEX